BREADCRUMBS AND BANANA SKINS

THE BIRTH OF THRIFT

JACQUELINE PERCIVAL

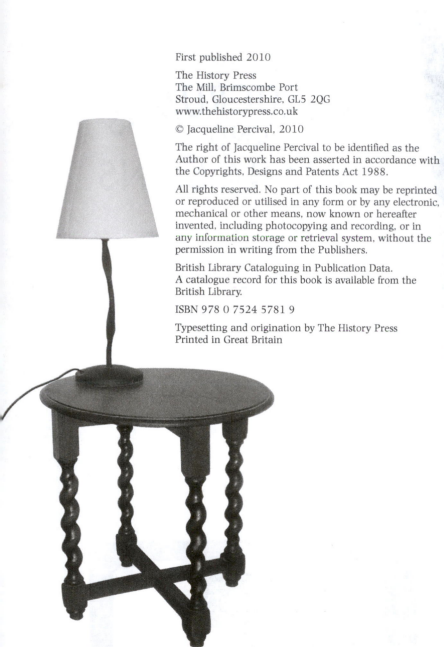

First published 2010

The History Press
The Mill, Brimscombe Port
Stroud, Gloucestershire, GL5 2QG
www.thehistorypress.co.uk

British Library Cataloguing in Publication Data.
A catalogue record for this book is available from the
British Library.

ISBN 978 0 7524 5781 9

Typesetting and origination by The History Press
Printed in Great Britain

Contents

Acknowledgements

Thanks go to lots of people: Robbie, Tina, Graham, Doris, Meredith, Robert, Ann Cutting and May for gifts of books; Amy Oldham for lectures on 'wetting the soap', recipes, dripping toast and hay box facts; Ethel Reeves for sharing food memories; Angie Thurley for memories of W.G.R. Francillon; Spot for photos; Janet Few, my Open University tutor, for the initial idea; Liz Hall for taking time from her PhD to read and comment; Mike for technical support; Robert Smith of Adelphi Books, Southsea, and Liz Seeber of Liz Seeber Books, both of whom produced the right book at the right time over and over again; Penny and Betsy for encouragement; the Tech Guys at PC World Portsmouth, Novatech Portchester and Kroll OnTrack, all of whom saved my sanity during the January snow when my computer died; and Gosport Discovery Centre for employment, professionalism and friendship, especially Julie M for silence and Lynda D for pointing me towards databases at just the right moment. Thanks also to Nicola Guy of The History Press, who gave me the chance to pontificate in print.

This book is for Dad, who would have been tickled pink to see his daughter in print at last.

Introduction

Many people raised in the 1950s may remember uncomfortably lumpy sides-to-middles sheets, cut-down clothes or oversized clothes bought with an optimistic eye for 'growing into them'. They might also remember their mothers saving string and envelopes or – like mine – throwing fits because they committed the unpardonable bath time sin of 'wetting the soap'. They might link these childhood experiences with wartime and austerity shortages and conclude that their mothers had had to save string, make peculiar meals and fuss about soap because they had no choice during and after the war years.

What they might not realise is that their grandmothers and great-grandmothers had also been part of the thrift generation; many of them shopping, cooking and housekeeping on tiny budgets and with none of the technological and time-saving gadgetry that we take so much for granted today.

However, there are often hints or clues to a family's domestic past. There might be an old rag rug, a handwritten recipe for rabbit stew, or an old cookery book or magazine handed down through the generations. Not only are such family heirlooms a link to the past, they are often the only clues that our grandmothers had been thrifty and resourceful housekeepers in their time.

Thrift, a word that has gone out of fashion in the last fifty or so years, was more often than not applied to housewives as they were, both literally and metaphorically, the keepers of the keys. In their hands and brains lay the responsibility for the happiness, comfort and prosperity of the family. This was achieved, often with much struggle, via careful money management, frugal shopping and cooking, throwing away nothing that could possibly be useful – whether incorporated into the next meal or made into something new for the house – and recycling unwanted oddments into something else. If they had a little spare time or space, or could save a little money, they might also breed rabbits to sell, make jumpers, or run small agencies: there were many ways of adding to the family's income.

Old cookery books and books teaching housewifery skills are a unique source for clues of the domestic past. Many of them disappeared during the paper salvage drives of the Second World

War, but sometimes, probably because they were so useful around the house, they were hidden away and carefully kept for the future. Today, they can be seen both as redolent of old-fashioned standards (housework timetables and starched tablecloths are probably less in use today than in the past) and valuable cultural documents: no other source material takes us so forcefully back to the time of hay boxes, homemade polish and unwieldy coal ranges. Additionally, photos and illustrations show us a range of desirable objects – whether film star bedrooms shining with satin eiderdowns and pale paintwork, or kitchens packed with the most modern gas ovens, water softeners and cooks' cabinets.

Some of the books that survive today are multi-volume encyclopaedia-type works, enormously heavy, with sumptuous bindings, and illustrations and detailed advice on such matters as large-scale entertaining or maintaining a large house and its accompanying range of servants. Others were produced on a far humbler scale, concentrating simply on helping the housewife get the very best value for her money, whether by advising on seasonal produce, painting and decorating, or keeping a budget. Although many were produced by the book publishers of the day, the various newspapers – *Daily Mail*, *Daily Express*, *Lloyd's Weekly* etc. – also published their own guides and cookery books, and the writers, Mrs C.S. Peel, Elizabeth Craig, Matilda Lees-Dods, Florence Jack and D.D. Cottington-Taylor, were probably as well known to housewives then as Nigella Lawson and Elizabeth David are today. Ms Jack and Ms Cottington-Taylor were at various times editors of *Good Housekeeping* magazine, Ms Lees-Dods lectured worldwide on domestic matters, Mrs Peel wrote many books on homemaking and cookery based on her own experiences, while Ms Craig was one of the most prolific cookery writers of her day.

This book investigates the world of domestic thrift in the twentieth century before the Second World War. The title is an appropriate one because in the years before the welfare state, cheap food and our modern throwaway society, housewives had to ensure that they did save odd bits and pieces such as breadcrumbs and banana skins. They also had to watch every penny and spend money with care because wages were often low, unemployment was often high and many families had very little to live on after the essential bills were paid. Therefore people had no choice but to live resourcefully and within their means. The nineteenth century reality of the workhouse lingered well into the twentieth century and the Means Test acted as an equivalent deterrent in the 1930s. Moreover, our current preoccupation with cheap food and its imminent disappearance is nothing new. Government policies outlined in the early 1930s included new measures to raise prices of foodstuffs to agreed levels and to ensure that none of these foodstuffs sold for less than this agreed level, and to curb the unlimited flow of imported foods. This meant, according to one report, that although the population had been accustomed to a policy of cheap food, people would have no choice but to adapt to these higher prices. Housewives, inevitably, would have had to revise their already tightly maintained budgets and practice even greater economies.

Chapter One starts with money. Many husbands received their pay in cash weekly, and wives had to ensure that their housekeeping allowance covered every expense and bill, and hopefully left a little to put into savings now and then. Husband and wife were encouraged to set up a family budget every year and to work within its framework, adjusting figures where necessary to ensure that every eventuality was adequately covered. Many affluent households also had to count pennies – the trick was not to let anyone know about it. Here, the need for frugality was more carefully veiled, as families higher up the social scale and far more visible on the social radar had much more prestige to lose by a sudden descent into the humiliations of financial difficulties. A class of people accustomed to prompt and deferential service from their own servants, and endless credit and deference from tradesmen and shopkeepers would, in the event of money problems, have been the subject of gossip at the very least and ostracised by their peers at the very worst. Such behaviour may seem archaic and somewhat ridiculous today, but the social class system of the times functioned in such a way that everyone knew more or less which class they belonged to, and were aware that stepping out of line in any way might well have brought disgrace to the family. Dismissing servants because of financial reversals could well have led to awkward reprisals at employment agencies, and it is also probably true that many middle-class women had no idea how to cook a meal until they were left without servants. Even further up the social scale were women who were completely accustomed to ringing a bell to summon a servant to pick up something from the floor. Such women would have had enormous difficulties coping with a reduced income, with food shopping, or, as frequently happened during the First World War, being left to cope with the administration problems of running a large house. Families long accustomed to frugal housekeeping, small fires, simple meals, recycling and making do were most probably far more successful in this area than those who had no such experience. Housekeeping advice and cookery books were therefore written to cater for both ends of the spectrum, for people coping on tiny earnings to those struggling on huge incomes. Because the cost of living in earlier times is a complex matter far beyond the scope of this book, figures and budgets given are simply examples quoted from contemporary sources (which themselves were usually written for guidance only), and therefore not to be taken as actual true-to-life examples. In addition, the lag between writing and publishing means that in many cases prices and figures were out of date by the time they were available to the general public. The point of this book is simply to show the extent of the advice available to housewives on the general subject of thrift before the Second World War.

Chapter Two covers food and shopping. Although supermarkets as we know them did not exist in the UK much before the 1950s, there was a wide range of places to buy food, including corner shops, chains such as the Co-op, street markets and greengrocers. There were also specialist shops such as fishmongers and cheesemongers ('monger' is an old word for a dealer) as well as general grocery stores where a variety of goods could be bought in one place, and, as was often the case, delivered to the customer's home later in the day. Shopping could be done by phone, in person at the shops or via the vans that travelled around the new housing estates.

Houses built between the wars were often massed into huge new estates miles from any shops, and housewives either had to trudge to and from the bus stop carrying heavy bags and baskets from shopping trips in the nearest town, or rely on the shop vans that sold bread, milk and other staples door-to-door. When shopping, housewives had to be careful to avoid the major pitfalls of the time such as dented tins, adulterated food or mud that added weight to 1lb of potatoes. They also had to ensure that they were buying nutritious food for

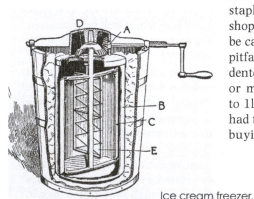

Ice cream freezer.

Refrigerator,
1920s.

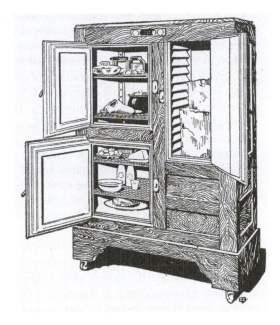

economical yet healthy meals: on a tiny budget it was essential to put
every penny to maximum use.

Finally, they had to ensure that they had adequate storage facilities
at home so that the food did not go off before it was cooked. Domestic
refrigerators were available but expensive in the 1930s, and because
of the vagaries of the British summer it was generally seen as a waste
of money to buy something that would only be used a few times
a year. Houses generally had a slate or stone shelf, or a stone floor,
where perishable food could be stored before use, and there were
various, reliable, old-fashioned devices such as channelled butter
coolers, meat safes and the old standby, a wet cloth draped over cheese
to keep it fresh. Many writers, aware that modern technology was
not universally available, continued to recommend the traditional
methods; indeed, it was often felt that the old methods of keeping
food fresh were actually the best. As contemporary technology was
not always totally reliable – and the refrigerators of the time had very
little actual storage space, being used mainly by affluent households
keen on impressing their peers with evidence that they could afford to
serve ice-cream and iced desserts – this approach was probably both
diplomatic and practical.

Chapter Three goes into some detail about contemporary food prices and food budgets, discusses actual menus, how various items were cooked, and how it was possible to save money in the kitchen by careful use of time, fuel and leftovers. Many households also had to cater for children, invalids and elderly people, and each group was seen as needing a different diet to the rest of the family. Of course, such variations could not always be accommodated, and many children ate what the rest of the family ate. Those families able to provide alternative food for their children were then faced with working out exactly what was nutritious and what was not, according to the dietary recommendations of the time. For example, at various times sausages might be avoided completely because their contents were suspect, or they might be provided only on special occasions, or offered freely on Sundays – every writer offered a different opinion.

This bland and dull diet – enlivened by periodic bursts of party and festive food – evolved as a supposedly safe middle course and may well have helped to make the British middle classes into unadventurous and uncomplaining eaters. It also no doubt caused a lot of children to have upset stomachs and bilious attacks following birthday or Christmas parties – an unaccustomed sudden intake of rich food would inevitably disrupt a child's system if it was more used to plain food. Mothers anxious to get food into a fussy eater might follow the example of the 1930s cookery books and call everyday dishes by exciting new names, thus hoodwinking the child into believing that they were eating something new and different. Christmas was seen as a particularly special time, and many housewives made plans and saved up for months to be able to provide festive food on Christmas Day. The actual cooking started in October when the new stocks of dried fruit appeared in the shops, and housewives were encouraged to make their Christmas puddings, cake and mincemeat well in advance. For those on particularly tight budgets, puddings could be made without eggs, sugar or suet and with lots of breadcrumbs to bulk them out. Cookery books published during and after the First World War sometimes included 'mock food' – dishes made from cheap ingredients but intended to taste like something more luxurious, such as pork or goose. For example, mock pork could be made from haricot beans, and mock goose from a combination of apple, sage, and onion and liver. During the Second World War, as Nicola Humble has pointed out, the emphasis shifted instead to the appearance of the dish.[1]

During and after the First World War there was a vogue for what might be called 'patriotic food', and some of these dishes are listed in Chapter Three. Stockpots, cooking mornings and alternative cooking methods such as hay boxes, chafing dishes and paper bags are also discussed, as well as the wide range of advice offered under the general heading of 'leftovers and the avoidance of waste'. Wasting food was seen as totally reprehensible (during the First World War it was seen as a crime), and cookery books went to great lengths to offer advice and recipes for using up tiny scraps of food such as breadcrumbs and drops of gravy.

Chapter Four covers the wider area of domestic thrift involving careful use of resources. Accustomed as we are today to throwing things away rather than mending them or making them into something else, it is surprising and sometimes humbling to learn about lighting fires with dried potato peelings or making bodkins out of broken boot laces. Books were often used as notebooks, door stops or pan trivets, and empty pages were torn out for letters, firelighters or for mopping up spills. Sometimes the bindings themselves were removed as contributions to wartime paper salvage drives. All sorts of oddments could be recycled and reused, from burst hot water bottles to broken diamanté necklaces. Although hoarding was not recommended, it was seen as reasonable to store a few potentially useful oddments for making gifts or repairing household items, clothes and shoes. Men seeking employment in the Depression years had to be well turned out and neatly dressed, and wives were encouraged to act as valets and to keep their clothes neat and tidy. Clothes too worn to repair could be recycled into clothes for babies and children or made into bedding and rugs, and eventually they could be bundled up and sold to the rag-and-bone man, who in turn sold them on to paper manufacturing firms.

Chapter Five covers the years of the First World War, when some of the most stringent economies of all were forced on the British public. Food shortages affected many people although rationing did not start until the year the war ended, and shortages of other kinds brought hardship to many. Everything from firewood to saucepans was scarce for some years following the end of the First World War, and people had to learn how to survive in such hard times. For many families life would never be the same again. Death duties, the loss of breadwinners, sweethearts and family members, and major financial setbacks meant that large homes might be partially closed, shared with other people or shut up for good. Women returning from active service in the war may well have decided that they would no longer be shut up with servants and housework and would forge new paths for themselves.

Many middle-class families found themselves forced to 'retrench', to drastically cut down their standards of living, and new patterns of family life evolved from these new beginnings. Contemporary cookery books are full of recipes for 'substitutes' for sugar and potatoes, and hints on saving bread, soap and fuel. Some ideas were less than useful – one (perhaps apocryphal) government directive urged people to collect acorns but omitted to tell them what to do with them once they had been collected. A similar process of confusion seemed to pervade the advice literature of the immediate post-war period. Some writers, appearing to ignore the previous four years, continued to write as if domestic life would quickly resume its pre-war tenor of servants, prosperity and middle-class serenity, while others bemoaned the loss of the past. Some, however, started to take careful stock of the situation and began to plan for a completely new and different future. Consequently, the advice manuals of the late 1920s and 1930s began to focus more on the perceived sanctity of marriage, the family and the role of the housewife as combined consumer/expert. At the same time the idea of labour saving began to creep into the literature as writers encouraged housewives to count steps, reorganise their kitchens and paint their brass taps with lacquer. Alas, they also began to urge housewives to spend fourteen hours a day on housework and encouraged levels of cleaning and tidying that were not far from insane, but that, as they say, is another story...

Chapter Six concerns the role of housewives as wage earners prior to the Second World War, concentrating on 'womanly' crafts and the general area of women and domesticity. Although the husband was traditionally seen as the family breadwinner and there was a certain pride attached to the fact that a wife of the middle classes was not expected to work outside the home, it is clear from the huge variety of money-making schemes available in contemporary magazines (plus much detailed information in homemaking literature) that many of them used their skills and experiences to good purpose inside the home. Other women may have been forced to contribute or even take total responsibility for the family income because of the illness or death of the main breadwinner. Money-making schemes targeted at women were often linked to traditional female attributes such as caring and nurturing, or skills such as sewing, mending and cooking. Others offered women the chance to try something new, to train for a job or career, or simply to earn their own pocket money.

Contemporary magazine small ads were rife with florid testimony, wildly exaggerated claims and levels of accuracy that nowadays might be best described as casual. No Trades Descriptions Act or Office of Fair Trading existed to investigate their murky world and consequently many of the examples that appeared in contemporary magazines were, like the unscrupulous shopkeepers of the period, to be avoided or approached with some degree of caution – *caveat emptor* ('let the buyer beware'). Information on money-making schemes in housekeeping manuals and hobby guides was often provided by an expert in the field, whether bee-keeping or sweet making, and on a wide range of ideas including (inevitably) cooking and catering, but also branching out into journalism, running agencies and craft work. A modern reader might be forgiven for thinking that a world of possibilities was open to a housewife with a small amount of money, a bit of spare time and a few friends. However, the reality was probably more a matter of trying to convince a sceptical husband that his dinner would still be on the table on time and constantly having to find new circles of acquaintances who would regularly buy the doughnuts or the playing cards.

Jacqueline Percival, 2010

one

Money

One of the problems experienced by housewives, particularly those of small means, was that of 'making the money go round'. Staying within the housekeeping budget by living as frugally as possible has always been a painstaking, laborious and worrying business. George Orwell's comment that the less money a person had to spend on food, the less they felt inclined to spend it on wholesome food would not have gone down well with the thousands of housewives wishing to provide nutritious meals for their families but forced to operate within the severe financial constraints of the times.[2]

Advice was available from a wide variety of sources, including magazines, cookery books and housekeeping advice books. Although no reader would have taken every word as gospel, such sources were useful to housewives of small means. Research by William Crawford on food and cooking in the 1930s showed that many housewives – especially those lower down the social scale – still preferred to cook in the traditional 'instinctive' style of their forebears, with only a small percentage using printed cookery books such as *Tried Favourites* or *MacDougall's*.[3] Higher up the social scale, books such as 'Mrs Beeton' were popular, although it's possible that more than a few 'Mrs Beetons' languished unused on kitchen shelves after being given to new brides as wedding presents; many families might have possessed one but perhaps used it only rarely. However, the sheer number of early twentieth-century cookery/housekeeping advice books surviving today gives us some idea of what was available to contemporary housewives. Some books included advice on setting up a workable family budget, the way to allocate the income to cover all expenses, how to keep accurate household accounts, and reminders about paying the bills on time. Remaining solvent was a matter of constant attention to pennies and shillings and hoping that the pounds would look after themselves.

Setting Up the Family Budget

Incomes varied dramatically, both within and across the various levels of the upper working and lower middle classes. In 1906 a middle-class family might have had anything between £200 and

£2,000 per year to live on; in 1924 a similar figure might have been between £500 and £1,500; and in the 1930s somewhere between £200 and £500 was seen as a fairly standard middle-class income. Working-class incomes varied even more widely. A government report from 1918 referred to working-class weekly wages as ranging from 25-40s per week in 1904, while William Crawford's 1937 investigations put 20-30s per week as an average wage.[5] Many families had no choice but to live as best they could under the circumstances. The important thing was for the housewife to be that ideal of domestic writers, 'a good manager'. However, as housewives past and present will readily agree, good management depends very much on what there is to manage. If the income was small or if there were particular unavoidable expenses – medical bills, growing children or high rent – it was very difficult to spread it appropriately.

Advice was readily available. Magazines, housekeeping advice books and some cookery books included information on managing money, keeping accounts, and paying household bills. The smaller the income, the greater the need for thrift and stringent economy. Many households enjoying a higher standard of living before the First World War were forced into economising during the 1920s and 1930s, and advice reflects this altered status, particularly in books aimed at the middle classes. Women had to learn to cook and do their own housework and gardening, sort out their own shopping and domestic problems, and do all the things that in more prosperous times had been done by servants.

Research published in 1937 pointed out that over 60 per cent of Britons' incomes pre-1929 were less than £125 per year, and less than 13 per cent were over £250 per year, with the average income being somewhat under £200.[6] Given these figures, it is all the more impressive that British housewives managed to feed their families and keep their homes ticking over as efficiently as they did.

Money management was also known as budgeting. In its simplest form, a budget is a price list and its function is to ensure that expenditure stays within income. Micawber-style warnings against the follies of overspending appeared many times in housekeeping advice books, and were particularly relevant for housewives coping on small allowances: the lower the income, the greater the need for careful budgeting.

Managing Money

The time-honoured way of ensuring that every expense was covered was to copy commercial bookkeeping methods of allocating money to various categories. These categories, known as the 'division of income', usually comprised:

- Rent, rates and taxes
- Food
- Household expenses
- Clothing
- Education
- Washing
- Medical bills
- Servants' wages (if applicable)

There were many variations on this basic list. Sometimes rent was paid by the husband; the wife might pay only the food and laundry bills or she might do some or all of the washing at home; the family might have reduced their food bills by keeping chickens or growing their own vegetables and fruit. The point was that the household sorted out a workable practical budget based on a balance between income and outgoings, and used it to monitor spending over a period of time.

Division of income varied widely according to class, income, location, number in the household, etc., and in the 1920s the figures used for a middle-class household might have looked like this:

Income example (1927, income = £500)

- £110 – rent
- £137 10s – food and household expenses
- £37 10s – service (servants' wages)
- £62 10s – dress
- £25 – health
- £37 10s – amusements
- £30 – education
- £50 – savings
- £10 – miscellaneous

Total: £500 [7]

This is approximately £9 a week. In contrast, a family living on the dole in the 1920s might have had to live on £1 12s 6d a week, with

6s used for rent, 2s for coal and light and 16s 6s for food (4s 1½d per person per week).[8] A tight budget for two people in the 1930s (income of £200) might have included £52 rent, £67 food, and £15 heat and light.

Successful Budgeting

A lot of juggling was necessary when the income was very small. Responsibility generally fell to the wife, as she was the person most concerned with the everyday bills and expenses. A married couple living on £200 per year in the mid-1930s had to perform major feats of financial organisation to stay solvent, and the housewife would have to stick to an extremely careful budget. This included keeping her surroundings clean, ensuring that the breadwinner stayed healthy and decently dressed at all times, and making use of every thrifty tip that came her way, simply for basic survival. She also had to know how to allocate every penny as economically and as wisely as possible for well-balanced, nutritious meals – an allocation of £67 per year for food equals just over £1 per week for two people – and how to use up all leftovers.

Juggling with small sums of money has never been easy. Dividing the allowance into five portions – fruit and vegetables; eggs, fish and meat; cereals and bread; dairy produce; bacon, fats, jam and other groceries – was seen as the best way to ensure value for money and maximum nutrition.[9]

Constant struggle seems to have been the norm for housewives with small budgets. Moving from a slum area to a modern estate could mean higher rents and travel expenses, but because these extra expenses cut into a budget that was probably already strained as far as it would go, the only way to factor them in was to reduce the food budget. Saving money on laundry bills by doing the washing at home after a baby's birth could result in major health problems for the new mother, and anyone with aspirations towards a better standard of living was forced to use all their energy scrimping, saving and economising in every possible direction.

Walter Greenwood's survey of late 1930s working-class life found that many people lived in poverty. One interviewee, a young working-class wife, felt that 'Nobody… can live a reasonably comfortable life on … less than five pounds a week'.[10] Her husband earned £3 18s per week (approximately £260 per year) and gave her £3 5s to cover household and living expenses. They had a new baby and a mortgage, and she was accustomed to thrift but resented the endless slog that went with it. Her methods of food shopping were similar to those recommended in the advice books of the time:

- She kept expenditure on meat down to 6-8d per day
- She used cheaper imported eggs for cooking (1½d each)
- She used a dozen eggs per week for eating (2s 1d)
- She bought 1lb of bacon, and 1½lb of butter per week
- She bought 4s worth of fruit and vegetables (cheaper at a market stall) every week
- She bought 1½ pints of milk per day
- She baked her own bread (1s 6d per week for flour and yeast)

Her weekly budget comprised:

- 17s – mortgage and rates
- 4s – coal (2cwt per week)
- 1s 6d – gas and electricity
- 30s – general groceries and meat
- 2s 11d – milk
- 5s – clothes (made her own)
- 2s – household replacements
- 1s – amusements (two cinema seats, 6d each)
Total: 63s 5d (balance banked)

Household Accounts

Once the household budget was set, it was up to the family to keep it going. Husband and wife usually kept their own separate accounts and combined them at the end of the month, the wife keeping track of her day-to-day expenses by means of one of the systems recommended in advice books or magazines.

Using a cheap exercise book ruled into vertical columns, a housewife could log her spending over a year, compare the results with the accounts of the previous year and then decide whether or not she needed to make any economies in the following year. On a more immediate level, she could check on the previous week's bill from the butcher, remind herself of the price of coal, or see when the children had had new shoes. Rather than relying on memory when she was out shopping, she was advised to carry a little notebook so she could jot down details of anything she bought or paid for with cash. On her return home (and if she remembered and had time to do such things), she would transfer these figures to her cash book, and at the end of the week she would add up her totals and transfer them to a weekly book. At the end of every month she would transfer these figures to a monthly book, and so on right through the year. By this point she would have a clear idea of the amounts spent on food, coal, gas etc., and could then make any necessary adjustments for the following year.

Some writers advised setting aside a regular time every month for dealing with the accounts and squaring up figures. If one partner forgot a sum or put something in the wrong column, they might both then spend time backtracking and hunting through lists of figures until it all 'came out right'. At the end of every year the entire budget was overhauled and any alterations made so that a new budget would be in place for the new year.

Budget example for an upper-middle-class household (1927, £6 12s 9d allowance for week, including £1 for 'personal')

- 16s 10d – butcher
- 4s 8d – baker
- 7s 6d – fish and poultry
- 9s 4d – dairy produce
- 7s – greengrocer
- 12s 6d – groceries
- £1 – servants' wages
- 8s 6d – laundry
- 10s 3d – sundries
- £1 2s 9d – personal

Total: £5 19s 4d (8d saved – note personal allowance overspent by 2s 9d)[11]

MODERN HINT

Keep track of direct debits and standing orders with a simple monthly budget laid out in an exercise book under vertical headings such as phone, gas and television licence, and horizontal headings January to December. A second book, covering regular payments such as paper bills, clothes, vet bills etc., is also useful. Total up each column and be amazed at the amount of money that goes out of the average bank account over a year. Check bank statements every month to ensure that payments are accurate and up to date and that outdated standing orders have been cancelled.

Paying the Bills

Payment for goods delivered to the house (as distinct from those bought in person by the housewife) were made either in cash at the door at the time of purchase or by a system known as 'tradesmen's books'. A ticket, usually a handwritten delivery note, arrived with the goods and the value and weight of the delivery was checked carefully against the original order, which was duplicated in a small 'check-book' usually kept in the kitchen. The tickets were collected over the course of a week or a month until payment became due, and only after careful comparison and crosschecking was the bill then paid. One way to avoid disagreement was for the mistress of the house, rather than the cook or housekeeper (who would only have been employed in the more affluent households) to write and sign all orders and then leave them at the shop herself.

Housewives were constantly urged to be on their guard against unscrupulous tradesmen (new brides were seen as particularly easy prey) and to instantly protest or threaten to take their custom elsewhere if they were swindled or overcharged. There were various ways of paying shop bills, whether by cash at the time of purchase, by weekly bills, or by a monthly cheque (more convenient if the month's housekeeping money was paid into a bank account on a monthly basis). Shopping in person ensured that payment was made at the time of purchase, while paying weekly meant totalling up the amounts for the butcher, baker and greengrocer and paying each bill in person at the end of the week. A careful shopper would try not to exceed her budget for meat etc., as doing so would upset her calculations.

Shops were keen to retain customers and would often extend credit for particularly reliable customers, although most people were expected to pay at the time of purchase: this avoided any trouble associated with non-payments. The early twentieth-century Co-op ran a variety of payment systems, such as weekly credit, running accounts, a club system and hire purchase, at the same time urging its managers to encourage cash payments in order to deter customers from running up bills they might not be able to pay.[12]

Sometimes, perhaps inevitably, advice followed on the heels of painful personal experience. In her earlier career as a restaurant owner, one former cookery teacher had been declared bankrupt in 1894, having failed to attend to the financial side of her expanding business.[13] This would almost certainly have caused intense family and social embarrassment. However, it appears that she bounced back from this setback with some determination and success, turning instead to a career as a lecturer and writer and compiling a huge and comprehensive guide to middle-class domestic life based around the fundamental idea that money spent is money wasted unless it is laid out with appropriate care and organisation – a fitting way to simultaneously overcome her unpleasant financial experiences and pass on advice to other people.

two

Food and Shopping

Lists, Attitude, Organisation

Having organised her budget and apportioned her food allowance, the thrifty housewife was ready to do her food shopping in a methodical way to get the best possible value for her money. It is probably fair to say that food shopping was taken far more seriously in the past than it is today.

The first step involved enthusiasm for the job in hand. 'Marketing is a really exciting adventure,' trilled one writer in the 1930s, 'what can be more thrilling, when you think of it, than to sally forth armed with your purse as a little "power house"... with which to nourish your family?'[14] Doubtless the average housewife could think of much more thrilling adventures than shopping for food with not enough money, but such diversions, unfortunately, were not appropriate matter for housekeeping manuals. With enthusiasm stirred to an appropriate level, the second step was to make a list. This was no haphazard rush through the nearest shop but a carefully prepared list covering everything that would be needed for the next few days. As well as including all the necessary items and ingredients for meals, the list had to take into account variables such as season, weather, access to shops, available storage and food already on hand.

MODERN HINT

Make a list! Saves time, sanity and money. Keep a master list on the computer and print off copies as needed, adding recipe specifics in a different colour – this makes it easier to spot what you need to buy.

Strategic timing was important: an early appearance at the greengrocers for optimum choice of goods had to be balanced against turning up near closing time for handy bargains, but with the possibility of empty shelves or shortage of stock. Lettuce and salad ingredients were usually bought in time for tea, while herbs and seasonings were bought later in the day so as to be ready to add to the evening dinner: timing was therefore critical so as to ensure optimum freshness of food. Housewives were also reminded (as if they really needed to know) that they were responsible for organising, shopping for, cooking – and washing up – three to four meals a day, which is approximately 1,500 meals a year.

MODERN HINT

Keep a list of recipes that can be prepared really quickly and with a minimum of ingredients and washing up. Keep a shorthand pad and pen in a prominent place and threaten the family with dire consequences if they forget to note down the last packet of biscuits before it disappears into oblivion. Stick a poster of seasonal foods on a cupboard door.

Shops and Shopkeepers

Housewives were advised to be selective in their choice of shops, to compare prices, to shop in person rather than on the phone (unscrupulous shopkeepers were wont to unload slow-moving or less-than-fresh produce on unwary phone shoppers), and to pay cash wherever possible: running up huge bills usually caused nothing but ill feeling. Many households patronised the delivery vans that made regular rounds selling milk, bread, groceries, meat and fish. Sometimes, however, there was no choice but to get the bus to the nearest shops. As films such as *Brief Encounter* showed, a shopping trip could become a day out with all sorts of interesting diversions. A housewife's life could be very lonely if she lived on a new housing estate and had no friends or family nearby. A trip to town – changing library books, doing a bit of window shopping or meeting friends – would have made a lot of difference to her day.

Housewives probably used a combination of shopping methods. Shopping by phone (assuming that both the household and the shop had phones) was best reserved for 'emergencies'. Before wartime brought its own unique definition of 'emergency', the term was used to describe the arrival of unexpected guests, and etiquette demanded that guests should be welcomed and fed, whatever time they arrived. Some shops would offer to phone customers, but some writers felt this method led to extravagance and was to be avoided wherever possible. By the 1930s, many people enjoyed the convenience of buying milk and bread etc. from roundsmen driving shop vans. Dairymen often sold bread, groceries and provisions as well as milk and cream, or goods could be ordered from the shop to be delivered later in the day. Most housewives bought the bulk of their food supplies locally, preferring to shop where goods were fresh and enjoyed a brisk rate of turnover. Women acquired the habit of carrying a bag or basket during the First World War, and goods were either tipped straight in or wrapped up in layers of paper. Shopping in person was almost always the best method for fresh or perishable produce, or anything that needed any degree of examination before purchase.

Shop staff were expected to be polite, knowledgeable and patient in their dealings with customers, many of whom were – as customers invariably can be – overbearing, indecisive, bad mannered or just plain difficult. No discerning housewife would shop at the type of establishments where meat was flyblown, fish smelt unpleasant, fruit was bruised or mouldy and tins were rusty or dented, and no discerning shopkeeper would employ scruffy staff or leave windows unwashed and floors muddy.

One way to illustrate a point is to make a story about it, and the Kellogg Co.'s 1930s book entitled *Sam Smith: Grocer Extraordinary* is the story of the ups and downs of a small grocery store before, during and after the installation of Sam Smith as assistant. Advised by his observant friend Ann, he drags the shop out of its decline by sprucing up the décor, bringing in new ranges of goods, streamlining the bookkeeping and getting to know his customers' likes and dislikes. Before long, business is booming, overdue bills are paid and Sam takes over as owner of the once-ailing business that has become a profitable concern. Although the book was produced as a how-to guide for shop managers and is a little too glib to be realistic, there is plenty of guidance on the best and most profitable ways to run an urban grocery shop in the 1930s. During this period, shoppers were aided by measures such as the introduction of National Mark foodstuffs and shops, the Empire brand, the Pure Food Act, the grading of eggs and the labelling of meat with its 'origins' (i.e. what cut it was).

Supermarkets as we know them now did not exist in the UK at this time, so the housewife had access to a wide variety of food shopping outlets, which in itself meant that she had to deal with a wide range of shops and shopkeepers.[15] These might include the fish shop (or, if she lived on the coast, the fish market), the butcher/poulterer/game dealer, the baker/pastry cook, the dairy, the cheesemonger, the grocer and the greengrocer. Stores such as Sainsbury's, the Co-op, Maypole and Home & Colonial were very popular in the 1920s-1930s, and there were many corner shops and small shops in villages and small towns that sold everything. Independent shopkeepers generally worked hard to provide good service and produce, and to stay on good terms with their customers. They were often troubled by the threat of the 'multiples', and conscious also that their trade experience would not necessarily stand them in good stead against the lures of stores such as the Co-op. Here, cheese, meat, biscuits, fish, fruit, groceries and tea were sold all in one place. The early twentieth-century Co-op was particularly keen to train its staff well and to branch out into a wide variety of services. Its managers were trained in areas including grocery and provisions, butchering, sausage making, ham-curing, greengrocery and fruit, and fish and poultry. They also developed sidelines in areas as diverse as pharmacy, dairy, a café, textiles, jewellery, coal, laundry, boot repairing, upholstery, tailoring and drapery.

Food buying entailed far more care and expertise than is employed today. Housewives were expected to know how to test eggs for freshness, how to know when lettuce was past its best, when it was the new season for dried fruit such as currants and raisins, and how to recognise, choose and store game and rabbits (fur and

Egg tester, 1920s.

feathers attached). Contemporary novels often included references to housewives carrying parcels of meat wrapped in bloodied paper, or chunks of ice that thaw and drip during encounters with friends, or bits of fish that poke out from their wrapping or even, if lobster was on the menu, make attempts to escape from the basket. This indicates that a certain skill (and speed) was needed to choose fresh produce and to get it home before it started to go off or escape from its wrappings. Bones, fish heads, etc., would also have been considered part of the purchase as all the pieces that would today be discarded were added to stock or soup: old cookery books include recipes galore for using such 'leftovers'.

Nutritious and Sensible Buying

A good shopper would plan meals ahead and know what every item cost. An even better shopper would also have been flexible enough to change her mind if she came across any real bargains and to snap them up immediately, willing to alter her menus and her budget if necessary.

MODERN HINT

Buy only if the bargains are worth it — giant bags of flour or dried pasta have to be stored somewhere, and often the huge packs of biscuits are wolfed down at warp speed simply because there are so many of them. Decant what you need into tins and hide the rest until it's needed.

Timing was paramount: the housewife had to be poised ready to pounce at the right moment. She had to be mindful of the busy times of days (avoiding early closing and the period just before dinner), hopeful of finding fresh produce, and flexible enough to revise her list where necessary, aware of varying prices. At the same time she had to be mindful of the seasons (to take full advantage of the first deliveries of dried fruit, fresh vegetables, new potatoes, strawberries, etc.), and the weather (sultry weather made it difficult to keep perishables fresh). She would also do her best to keep on good terms with local shopkeepers (no one wanted the public humiliation of 'unpleasantness' with tradespeople and the shops had no desire to lose customers), and to pay promptly – using cash where necessary.

Planning and method were vital. 'Attractive, nourishing meals, depend quite as much on your intelligent actions in the shops as on your industry and skill in the kitchen.'[16] Some goods and staples were cheaper and more economical when bought in bulk: flour, lentils, dried beans and household basics such as soap and candles could be stored almost indefinitely, while coffee, tea and butter were best bought as needed in small quantities. Most of the shopping, including the traditional Sunday joint, could be done on Saturday.

Few homes had refrigerated storage space; housewives had to buy fresh and perishable produce for immediate use and ensure that it was stored in the coolest space available. Those districts able to take advantage of the vans selling bread and dairy produce door-to-door could, by the 1930s, rely on produce being hygienically packaged in tins, waxed paper or cardboard boxes. This automatically led to a more accurate system of standardisation, and this in turn allowed housewives to work out their recipes more precisely. A 4oz package was more likely to be 4oz than the old-fashioned and vague instructions to take a handful of flour or a nut of butter. It might also be the case that accurate measures and precise instructions took away some of the spontaneity and charm of the old recipes. However, it certainly made them more reliable and easier for novices to tackle, a state of affairs that benefited many women during and after the First World War.

According to research in the 1930s, the average amount spent on food per head per week was just under 9s.[17] These figures derived from a survey that divided the retail money value of the UK's total food supply in 1934 by the population. Some people enjoyed a better than average diet while many others did not. First of all, housewives were encouraged to map out a rough menu to cover the next few days before comparing prices in the various shops they patronised. The next step was to make out a shopping list, with due regard for bargains and seasonal items. Next they were advised to allocate their food money according to the five main food groups (fruit and vegetables; eggs, fish and meat; bread and cereals; milk and cheese; bacon, fats, jams and other groceries) to ensure optimum nutritional value for money. Finally, having done the morning's housework, they could set out for the shops.

MODERN HINT

Internet shopping saves time, fuel and temper. Organic boxes of vegetables can be ordered and delivered on a regular basis. One vanload from a supermarket can transport the equivalent load of five or six cars.

Caveat Emptor (Let the Buyer Beware)

Shopping was not simply a matter of steering a trolley around the nearest supermarket and collecting everything in one go, as modern shoppers are accustomed to do. Because storage problems beset both houses and shops (many houses lacked electricity and adequate cupboard space, and older houses frequently harboured mice, silverfish or cockroaches), some foodstuffs were bought daily, some less regularly. Everything – even packaged goods – had to be examined, checked for freshness or purity, and where possible sampled before purchase to ensure flavour, freshness and freedom from adulteration. Some books suggested decanting all foodstuffs from paper bags into cans or jars as soon as they arrived in the kitchen to reduce the risk of infestation by pests. Pricelists were available at most shops so women could compare prices and special offers. However, most food shopping was done at local shops where the range of goods and services was familiar and known to be reputable: only the most experienced shoppers, it was said, could afford to shop in anything but the very best stores.

Good hygiene was essential. Before the First World War women were urged to inspect dairies in person and to insist that their milk was delivered in sealed bottles. As one writer pointed out: 'The proper hygienic delivery of our food is not sufficiently insisted on, and if mistresses themselves were only more particular on this point the tradespeople would be obliged to conform'.[18] Other foodstuffs that needed to be carefully chosen and stored came from the following outlets:

- Baker: new bread was seen as extravagant because it was difficult to cut thinly when fresh. It was also thought to be hard to digest new bread so it was best to order it a day before it was needed

- Butcher: unpleasant-smelling meat was to be avoided at all costs. Pork was best bought only from the most reliable butchers
- Game merchant: plucked birds were examined to ensure the flesh and colour points were satisfactory. Viewed undressed, as it were (without feathers), a better indication of freshness was possible
- Fishmonger: fish prices fluctuated in the 1930s, varying by 3-4*d* per lb. Fish smelling strongly of iodine was best avoided
- Dairy: butter had to be 'dry', that is, not packed in water to increase its weight. Milk was best bought in sealed bottles. Cheese was sampled before purchase
- Grocer: dented or rusty cans were best avoided. Dried fruit was best bought when new stocks arrived in autumn (perhaps one reason why Christmas cakes and puddings were made in autumn). Dried figs were sometimes infested with small maggots. Coffee and tea were sampled before purchase
- Greengrocer: products bought 'in season' were always freshest and best

Vegetables were sold pre-washed and partially trimmed by the 1930s so housewives were less likely to be paying for mud and unusable outer leaves (although in former times peelings and leaves would have been put into the stockpot). Fresh produce was best bought early in the day – stocks were not replenished as speedily as they are today, and no-one wanted the wilted lettuce or green potatoes rejected by other more discerning shoppers. Fruit from all parts of the world was available (for a price) in the 1930s, although soft fruits such as strawberries were not imported right through the year as they are nowadays.

Eggs were a complicated commodity. They were available as imports or home-produced, as cracked or intact, to be used fresh or preserved for later use. For various reasons to do with collection and transport, imported eggs were best for cooking and home-laid ones were best for breakfast, but 'cooking' eggs could be used when English ones were expensive. The only reliable way to test for freshness was to crack them open and examine them individually on a saucer. Other methods entailed shaking them (bad ones rattled), holding them up to a light (stale ones had dark spots), or floating them (stale ones turned on their ends). Stale eggs were lighter than fresh but it was not easy to tell the difference. Bridget Williams has pointed out that in the late nineteenth century, home-produced eggs ʾre often past their best because farmers were not always careful about getting them to market while they were fresh.[19] National Mark eggs were seen as reliable, and eggs for preserving were best bought fresh from the nest. Eggs could be preserved for use later on, and various preservatives such as water-glass were available in the shops. However, water-glass made shells brittle so eggs preserved this way could not be successfully boiled – they were fine for general cooking and baking, however.

National Mark Products

An early example of 'buying British', the National Mark scheme was introduced in the early 1930s and supervised by the Ministry of Food. Products bearing the National Mark logo were guaranteed to be pure and of good quality: it was thus seen as a reliable brand at a time when a lot of the foodstuffs in circulation were of more dubious quality. It was also said to benefit the inexperienced housewife: cuts of meat, frequently a mysterious area of marketing for the uninitiated, were labelled with their 'origin' (cut). Buying readymade foods such as jam and bottled fruit saved both time and money. Jam making and fruit bottling were messy, labour-intensive jobs and many housewives would have agreed that the time buying jam and bottled fruit was time well spent. By the mid-1930s the range of products was wide and comprehensive, including these:

- Tinned fruits: apples, blackberries, blackcurrants, cherries, gooseberries, strawberries, loganberries, plums, damsons, greengages, and redcurrants
- Bottled fruits: rhubarb, mixed apple and blackberries, plus all the above except strawberries
- Tinned vegetables: stringless beans, carrots, peas, spinach, mixed vegetables, beetroot, celery and new potatoes
- Bottled vegetables: asparagus, beetroot, turnips, beans, peas and mixed vegetables
- Jam: blackberry, cherry, gooseberry, loganberry, quince, redcurrant, blackcurrant, damson, greengage, plum, raspberry and strawberry
- Dairy products: creamery butter, Caerphilly, Stilton and Cheshire cheeses
- Other products: honey, cider, perry, flour, poultry, beef and eggs [20]

Eggs were graded into four groups (pullets weighed 1½oz, mediums weighed 1¾oz, standards weighed 2oz, and specials weighed 2¼oz) and candled (held up to a light to ascertain freshness). Housewives therefore knew that National Mark eggs were fresh and that they were getting value for money as specials cost more than standards. The opening of a National Mark shop in London in 1931 meant that a wide range of goods of a consistent quality were available to shoppers. The range of products itself was regularly inspected and policed by the government, and the findings and recommendations made available in the form of HMSO leaflets.

Food Adulteration

Inexperienced housewives, such as new brides, were often seen as easy prey for unscrupulous shopkeepers. They were less likely to be able to spot sharp practices such as short weight (15oz rather than 16oz), mistakes in reckoning up bills, and cutting on the 'wrong side' of the fingers (an old drapery trick to make 1yard equal less than 36in). Housewives and other shoppers also had to beware of the much more worrying problems associated with food adulteration.

The early twentieth-century housewife had to steer a careful and vigilant course through the murky seas of adulterated foodstuffs. Housewives were urged to buy the best they could afford and regularly check for adulteration. Inferior products were more expensive in the long run, and in any case some of the adulterants were toxic (see John Burnett, *Plenty and Want*). The 1910 edition of *Enquire Within* includes a long list of the adulterations highlighted by the Sale of Foods and Drugs Act, including the following:

- Bread: alum (used as a whitener but also enabled bakers to use inferior flour), borax, sulphate of copper, chalk, bran, potatoes
- Butter: made heavier by the addition of water
- Cayenne pepper: brick dust, red lead and vermilion (both toxic)
- Coffee: ground acorns
- Pepper: sand, seed husks, dust 'of a variety of descriptions' [21]
- Sausages: best avoided due to the (rumoured) addition of unpleasant oddments of various kinds
- Tea: indigo, plumbago and French chalk [22]

Furthermore, the hygiene and purity of the household water supply was often uncertain, with domestic cisterns rumoured to contain foreign bodies such as soot, dead mice and cockroaches. Householders were expected to keep their cisterns covered and clean – local authorities took no responsibility for this.

Food adulteration was as much of a problem to reputable retailers such as the Co-op as it was to their customers. The Co-op carried out stringent quality tests on foodstuffs such as arrowroot, butter, cinnamon, cloves, flour, ginger, mustard, olive oil, sugar and tea, and was constantly alert to ensure that their products were adulterant-free.[23]

By the 1930s the laws concerning food adulteration had been tightened up to the extent that certain substances, such as artificial colourings, were permitted under certain conditions. Substances such as ground fruit stones (used to bulk out spices and pepper) or water (to dilute milk) were no longer allowed. However, certain food preservatives were essential during storage and transit from abroad. Benzoic acid and sulphurous acid were the only two preservatives permitted, while boracic acid was no longer used as it was said to be harmful if ingested heavily – people who ate a lot of processed food would probably have been at risk. Boracic/boric acid was better known in the 1930s as a mild lotion for ailments such as sore eyes, or as a dusting powder or antiseptic.[24]

Food Prices

Modern anxiety about rising food prices is nothing new: cookery and housekeeping advice books published in the 1910s-1930s were full of advice on getting the best value from every penny. Food prices were a worrying part of life for all classes and incomes, a fact reinforced by the number of budgets and economy drives printed in middle-class magazines such as *Good Housekeeping* – proof that even the middle classes had financial problems. Families on low incomes were particularly at risk from price rises but, on the other hand, such families often had more practical experience of surviving hard times than their more affluent peers.

Food prices 1910s (pre-war period)
- Fish (per lb except where stated): brill, 6d-10d; cod, 6d; Dover sole, 1s 6d; haddock, 4d; hake, 4d-8d; lemon sole, 8d-1s; plaice, 6d-8d; sea bream, 6d-8d; skate, 4d-6d; turbot, 10d-1s 6d; whiting, 3d-8d; mackerel, 4d-8d each; red mullet, 8d each; smelts 3s-4s per dozen

- Dried fish: fresh herrings, 1½d-2d each; haddock fillets, 6d per lb
- Shellfish: lobsters, 2s (very small); scallops, 1s-2s 6d per dozen; shrimps, 4d per quart
- Vegetables (per lb): Brussels sprouts, 1½d-2½d; Spanish onions, 1½d-2d; salsify, 8d; cauliflower, 3d-6d each
- Salad vegetables: cucumber, 3d-6d each; forced lettuces, 2d-4d each; tomatoes 8d per lb; watercress, 1½d-2d per bunch
- Fruit: apples, 2d per lb; bananas, 1d-1½d each; Jaffa oranges, 2d-4d each; pears, 2d-3d each; pomegranates, 2s each; strawberries, 4d-1s; tangerines, 1s per dozen
- Groceries: baking powder, 1d per packet; caster sugar, 2d per lb; chocolate powder, 8d per lb; coffee, 1s 4d per lb; eggs, 1d each; flour, 1d per lb; marmalade, 4d per lb; pineapple, 5½d for a small tin; tea, 1s 6d per lb
- Dairy: butter, 1s 9d for 1½lb; milk, 2d per pint
- Meat (per lb): brisket, 7½d-8d; Canadian ham, 7d; lard, 8d; leg of mutton, 10d; pork chop, 1s 6d; ribs of beef, 9½d; suet, 5d-8d; kidneys, 3d each; ox tail, 1s 6d-1s 9d each
- Breads: Bath bun, 1d each; bread, 3d each; brown bread, 2d each; seed cake, 6d[25]

The years 1934-1937 saw the publication of several studies on public health, nutrition and food supply, including research by John Boyd Orr, Margery Spring Rice, G.C.M. M'Gonigle and J. Kirby, and G.D.H and M.I. Cole. By this time the era of cheap food was almost at an end and new food policies were being formulated to protect UK agriculture during a period of worldwide economic depression. This situation, to some extent, mirrors preoccupations with rising food prices in the early years of the twenty-first century. At the same time, a considerable proportion of the population was unable to afford good food and was at risk of being undernourished, and concern focused on the health of school children and families on low incomes. Cookery books began to appear with common-sense advice on shopping and cooking on a range of budgets, using thrifty recipes as before but now aimed at a wider range of readers. Food prices were sometimes included (see below) and it is possible to reconstruct a middle-class diet from the 1930s using a source such as Garth and Wrench's *Home Management* (1934). This can be compared to some extent with a working-class diet such as that outlined in Rice's *Working-Class Wives* (1939). It then becomes very apparent that the gap between the poor and the relatively comfortably off was far wider than it is today.

Food prices 1930s (post-First World War period)

- Fish (per lb): cod, 10d; kippers, 5d per pair; fresh herrings, 2½d each; plaice, 1s
- Vegetables (per lb): Brussels sprouts, 2d; carrots, 2d; peas, 3d; potatoes, 1d; cabbage, 2d each; cauliflower, 3d each
- Salad vegetables: tomatoes, 4d per lb
- Fruit (per lb): cooking apples, 2d; lemon, 1d each; oranges, 1d each; strawberries, 5d
- Groceries: baking powder, 1d per packet; blancmange, 6d per packet; butter beans, 3d per lb; cocoa, 1s per lb; coffee, 2s per lb; currants, 6d per lb; eggs (imported), 1s 3d per dozen; flour, 2d per lb; jam, 7d per lb; macaroni, 4d per lb; prunes, 8d per lb; rolled oats, 2½d per lb; sugar, 3d per lb; tea, 1s 8d per lb
- Dairy: butter 8d-11d per lb; cheese 8d-10d per lb; margarine, 8d per lb; milk, 3d per pint
- Meat (per lb): Danish bacon, 7d-1s 11d; ribs of beef, 1s 3d-1s 11½d; brisket, 10d-11d; chicken plus giblets, 2s 9d; English ham, 1s 5d-2s; lard (imported), 4d-7d; leg of mutton, 1s 10d-1s 11d; loin of pork 1s 3d; mutton chops 2s 7d-2s 8d; pig's fry 8d; pork sausages 1s 3d; rib of beef 10d; sheep's heart, 8d; beef suet, 6d; tripe, 8d; calf's head, 9d-11dd each
- Breads: bread (2lb loaf), 3½d; brown bread, 2d[26]

Meal Planning

Domestic writers took the subject of meal planning very seriously in the 1930s, and a great deal of information was available on topics such as the most efficient way to spend a food allowance, and how to do the sums for cost-per-head catering.

The amount allowed for food depended not only on the sum available but the number of mouths to feed and the family's social class and aspirations. A small family keen to cling to traditional middle-class patterns of eating (five meals a day, including teatime with bought cakes and meat for dinner every day) might spend more than a larger family eating three meals a day, having meat only once or twice per week and making bread and cake at home.

Cookery books were available for a variety of budgets, with authors taking great pains to include menus and advice that would help the housewife provide good meals for her family.

MODERN HINT

Make friends with your cookery book! Check out the public library and second-hand bookshops for basic cookery books. Photos and background chat make modern titles heavy and many are far too expensive to be used the way they should be – real cookery books should be stained and knocked about, with notes written against the recipes and pages that fall open at favourite sections. Celebrity chefs are not necessarily the most suitable people to write the basic cookery books that should be in everyday use.

Emelie Waller, author of a book aimed squarely at housewives on tight budgets, felt that 27s 6d per week was the smallest amount that could be allocated to feed two adults and three children. She provided very detailed shopping lists to cover a three-week period and pointed out that many families lived on much less. Even so, some of her recommendations seem to be extraordinarily tightly costed. However, she succeeded in offering menus for four meals a day including scrambled eggs, bean soup, baked apples and onion pie.[27]

Elizabeth Craig's *Economical Cookery* provided very precise guidance on meal planning. This meant varied and nourishing meals served in appropriate portions at regular hours (more for manual workers, less for those with sedentary occupations), planned well in advance and with good use made of leftovers. She provided a variety of specimen shopping lists priced at 30s (parents and one child), under 30s (parents and one child), £1 15s (parents and four children, living in a town), and £1 13s (parents and four children in the country). Her advice on thrifty eating included making use of cheap cuts of meat such as aitchbone of beef, neck of lamb and neck of mutton, using up leftovers and planning menus to cover a week at a time.[28]

Margaret Garth and Mrs Stanley Wrench provided advice for middle-class housewives catering for four people on 10s, 12s 6d, and 15s per head per week. They also gave a week's sample menus and provided a breakdown of recipes with prices showing, for example, how a sum of £1 18s might be spent. This included 1s 6d for a rabbit, 1lb of tomatoes for 4d, and fifteen eggs for 1s 10½d (½d each).[29]

Those housewives who were particularly interested in catering economy could cost out their menus to the halfpenny using a system derived from the business world: the cost-per-head system.[30] This comprised subtracting the weekly milk, bread and general grocery figure (tea, sugar, flour etc.) from the total sum available for food, and dividing the remainder by seven. This sum was divided into the four meals a day, and would cover items such as bacon and fruit for breakfast, eggs and vegetables for lunch, cakes and jam for tea, and meat and vegetables for dinner. Each meal was then divided into the amounts for meat, vegetables, etc., so the housewife knew exactly how much money was available. The various juggling involved with 'save' and 'splurge' could then be balanced, and as long as the basic figures were not disturbed it was possible to have treats such as strawberries or fresh pineapple. A slightly more extravagant meal one day might mean a frugal one the next, but ultimately the sums would balance as long as the initial calculations were correct.

Once the food was brought to the kitchen, the next job – cooking – began. For the housewife on a small budget this was a crucial part of her daily work and there was no shortage of information available to assist the inexperienced.

Cooking

three

Stores

The thrifty housewife would always maintain a good store cupboard. Ideally she would also know how to check for freshness in meat, fish, fruit, vegetables and dairy produce; how to store foodstuffs when they arrived in the kitchen; how to cook them economically; what convenience foods were worth buying; which surpluses were worth the financial investment; and the prices of a wide variety of foods, so that she could always keep within her budget while simultaneously juggling potential 'splurge' and 'save' possibilities. Country housewives were also expected to be able to take advantage of wild foods such as berries and nuts; know how to preserve eggs; and make use of whatever rural produce came their way, from a pail of dandelions to half a pig. A basic store cupboard might contain any of the following in the 1920s:

- Groceries: tea, coffee, cocoa, sugar (loaf, cooking, castor, brown), flour, rice, sago, tapioca, semolina, pearl barley, cornflour, ground rice, arrowroot, macaroni, oatmeal, haricot beans, butter beans, lentils, currants, sultanas, raisins, candied peel, almonds, angelica, preserved cherries, prunes and other dried fruit, gelatine, caraway seeds, desiccated coconut and golden syrup

- Condiments: salt, pepper, cayenne pepper, mustard (English and French), vinegar, tarragon vinegar, salad oil, Worcester sauce, anchovy sauce, tomato sauce, ketchup, Bovril or Oxo, gravy browning, capers, olives, curry powder, dried herbs (thyme, sage, parsley, marjoram), cloves, peppercorns, nutmeg, ginger, mace, cinnamon, flavouring essences (vanilla, ratafia, lemon, celery), cochineal, baking powder, carbonate of soda and cream of tartar

- Prepared foods: jams, marmalade, pickles, chutneys, fruit (tinned or bottled), jellies (tablet or bottled, varieties included strawberry, cherry, orange, blackcurrant and greengage), soups (tinned, bottled or tablet), anchovies, sardines, tinned salmon, tinned lobster, tinned meat (tongue, corned beef), potted meat and fish, tins of condensed milk, custard powder and biscuits

MODERN HINT

Decide what you need in your store cupboard and keep it stocked up.

Convenience Foods

Many of our modern convenience foods have their origin in the nineteenth century. Sometimes cookery books included adverts for new food products – providing the housewife with a useful memory jogger – as well as a picture, sometimes a price and, frequently, a florid testimonial from someone in the public eye.

By the 1920s housewives began to be taken seriously by advertisers as consumers and spenders. Advertising copy was frequently lurid, inaccurate or downright untrue, but many of the adverts from either side of the First World War would strike our modern eyes as distinctly attractive miniature social documents of their time. Convenience food adverts from this period include:

- Borwick's baking powder
- Bovril (originally Lemco)
- Cadbury's cocoa
- Cerebos table salt
- Chivers jam, jellies, canned fruits and custard powder
- Coomb's flour, custard powder, egg powder, baking powder and blancmange powder
- Edwards' desiccated soups (known as EDS, and costing 1½d a packet in 1920)
- Eglah dried egg powder
- Florador pastry flour
- Gordon Dilworth's tomato catsup
- Latham & Co's Cakeoma (cake mix)
- Messina Works' Yolkine
- Nelson's range of gelatine products, 1903
- Oxo
- Robertson's mincemeat and Silver Shred marmalade
- Robinson's patent barley
- Shippam's meat paste

These products would slowly but surely work their way onto shopping lists and into store cupboards simply because goods such

Advertisement for
Peterkin custard.

Are *YOU* using the following?

" PETERKIN "

REAL EGG CUSTARD POWDER
"The finest Custard Powder obtainable."
—*Grocers' Journal*, 2nd July, 1921.

" PETERKIN " *Blancmanges*

In all popular Flavourings.
Delicious—Dainty—Delightful.

" PETERKIN " *Patent Corn Flour*

Guaranteed perfectly pure, wholesome
and nourishing — very easily digested.
Excellent for thickening Soups, Sauces, etc.

" PETERKIN " *Self Raising Flour*

Milled from the finest wheats in the world.
Makes delicious Cakes, Pastry & Puddings.

*All the foregoing products manufactured
under ideal conditions in Scotland by*

THE "K.O." CEREALS CO. LTD.
LONDON   GLASGOW   GREENOCK

as packet jelly, meat paste, ready-sifted flour and pre-stoned raisins
made life easier for the housewife and speeded up her cooking by
no small degree. Why buy butcher's suet, skin and chop it yourself,
when Atora was skinned, chopped and ready to use? Pre-packaged
and pre-weighed ingredients also meant more precision and less
hit-and-miss weighing and measuring, especially when using
cookery books vague about weights and measurements.

There was also less waste with pre-packaged food, and this in
turn meant that the housewife could apportion her money more
efficiently. If, for example, a packet of Shredded Wheat was known
to last for a week she might, if she followed the cost-per-head plan,
be able to splash out on the odd small luxury with the money left
over from the breakfast allowance. Shredded Wheat was itself used
as an ingredient in thrifty recipes from the early 1930s: in one,
the insides were removed and they were buttered inside and out

and put to crisp in the oven. Then a mixture of chopped rabbit or lamb and 2oz of finely chopped ham were moistened with white sauce and put inside the biscuits and baked until hot. In the other, a beaten egg and a spoonful of milk were poured inside, a spoonful of white sauce poured on top, and they were baked until set, served with a rasher of bacon on top. Meals such as these were probably intended as a 'relish' for the male breadwinner – they are clearly too small to be anything more substantial.

The firm of Nelson & Co. produced a hugely popular cookery book that was free for the price of a stamp to advertise its own brand of gelatine-based products. The 1903 edition (the twenty-second) included recipes galore for dishes made with Nelson products, including jellies (both sweet and savoury), creams, and veal and ham pie. Cookery books sometimes included recipes using tinned food. John Burnett has pointed out that food canning had been around since the 1820s, and that by 1914 Britain imported more tinned food than any other country.[31] Cookery writers appear to have embraced the use of tins in daily cooking with guarded enthusiasm. Historically, tins had not been particularly safe, and even in the 1920s and 1930s the 'Mrs Beeton' books remained slightly aloof from their joys. Despite focusing on safety precautions – not using bulging or rusted tins and testing for copper by sticking a steel knife into a tin of fruit – they did concede that a good brand of prawns made a palatable curry, that tinned meat was handy on board ship, and that in emergencies tinned soup was a useful item to have in the cupboard.

However, by the 1930s tinned food was seen as safe and convenient for household use, and cookery books began to include recipes using commercially produced produce. As regards safety, it was explained that imported tinned goods were examined at the port of entry by local authority inspectors with powers to seize any inferior consignments, and that a new type of tin known as the 'sanitary tin' had been introduced.[32] These new containers were not soldered as they had been in the past, and their interiors were lacquered to better retain the natural colour of the contents. Tinned foods were so handy to have in store that it was seen as a good idea to know how to incorporate them in family meals. No longer was it seen as a sign of bad or lazy housekeeping if a housewife used the occasional tin. Asparagus, carrots, peas, peaches, salmon, sardines and lobster were all available in tins, as were baked beans – nothing so humble as the twentieth-century baked beans on toast but instead delicacies such as baked bean charlotte, baked beans and sausages, or fried suet pudding and baked beans. The acceptance of convenience foods such as tins may even have contributed to the increased leisure time and mobility of the working population. Housewives were no longer as tied to the kitchen and consequently might have enjoyed a little more time and leisure out of the house.

Housewives could also enjoy the convenience of fruits and vegetables grown at home or on their allotments. Many households did their own preserving, canning and bottling at home or using the equipment loaned by the Women's Institute, and by the early 1930s they could also take advantage of the government-operated National Mark scheme and buy English produce in the shops. As canning and preserving was hot and messy work, such initiatives would have been a boon to those housewives able to afford them.[33] Another handy form of convenience food available in the 1930s was quick-chilled fish. Sold by both fishmongers and grocers, they were displayed in showcases similar to modern chiller cabinets.[34] The thrifty housewife may have been able to buy such items, provided they were within her price range.

Yet another useful idea was to show the step-by-step way of following a recipe in a cookery book – particularly helpful for inexperienced cooks or fiddly recipes. In 1913, *Home Cookery & Comforts* ran a feature called 'Cookery Cinema', which appears to be a very early example of photo cookery, a method much used today to demonstrate step-by-step processes. The photos are clear enough for a modern reader to see exactly what is going on, and the accompanying captions are concise and easy to understand. By the 1930s, photos were being used to illustrate room settings, cookery processes and particularly modern kitchen and household equipment, such as gas ovens. Writing and photography became more firmly linked when cookery writers wrote oven cookery books, as with D.D. Cottington-Taylor's compilation of recipes for the Vulcan Stove Company in 1936. D.D. Cottington-Taylor, like Florence Jack before her, was a director of the Good Housekeeping Institute, and also a writer of books about housekeeping and cookery.

Sometimes cookery writers branched out in other directions, such as providing recipes using convenience foods. Elizabeth Craig, for example, was a familiar face to book and magazine readers searching for new recipes and ideas. As well as being a prolific author, she also co-designed a range of oven glassware for Phoenix and compiled various recipe books for convenience food producers such as Foster Clark.[35, 36]

Finally, it should be noted that although they were cheap and easy to use, convenience foods were not always within the financial reach of those who enjoyed them. *Home Cookery & Comforts* included this note from an impoverished but resourceful reader from Crouch End:

> I am very fond of baked beans with tomato sauce, but they cost 8½*d* per tin, which is more than I can afford. Instead, I get half a pint of haricot beans, soak them for twelve hours, then put them in a jar in the oven. When they are nearly done, I add to them a penny square of tomato soup (any good brand will do), and let them finish cooking. They are just as nice as any you can buy, but cost a great deal less.[37]

MODERN HINT

Read the labels and see if an equivalent can be made using the list of ingredients. Muesli, soup and nearly all biscuits and cakes are far cheaper made at home using this method, and will not contain artificial additives.

Economical Recipes

Housewives were expected to provide nutritious meals for the family with the minimum of financial outlay. Many families had to manage on very small incomes, and a wife's skills at marketing and cooking would have made a big difference to the family's wellbeing and standard of living. The old saying that says a wife can throw out with a spoon faster than a husband can throw in with a spade would have been very appropriate during this period.

Writers of cookery and advice books invariably made reference to the need for economy in the home, whatever level of income their readers may have enjoyed. For example, Matilda Lees-Dods, author of a particularly large and comprehensive guide for newlyweds of the upper middle classes, was at great pains to impress upon her well-heeled readers the absolute necessity for thrift and economy at the outset of married life. And, at the other end of the financial scale, a more modest publication such as *Home Cookery & Comforts* (a thirty-page monthly supplement to the magazine *Home Notes*) took the practice of thrift entirely for granted. Here, the everyday problems of domestic life were aired and discussed in the form of chatty articles and a sprinkling of handy hints sent in by readers. Advice was given on problems such as providing a Sunday dinner for 1s, making the best use of cheap meat such as a leg bone of beef (costing 2s 6d in November 1913), and how best to spend a fixed food allowance of £2 10s a week.[38] Between these two extremes were all the various degrees of income and aspiration that characterised the 'respectable' English household in the early twentieth century. One ultra-thrifty publication was the *You & I Cookery Book*. Subtitled, 'An effort to meet a need in the cheapest form', its recipes were very economical indeed:

- Savoury dish: two tomatoes cut up with 3oz of cheese and cooked in a dab of margarine, a few breadcrumbs added, the dish then served on toast
- Cooked nettles: young nettle leaves boiled in salty water for 30 minutes, and served with butter
- Tasty breakfast dish: a piece of cheese (specifically 5in by ½in), cut up and soaked in milk overnight, then boiled for three minutes and served on buttered toast with a few breadcrumbs stirred in[39]

Even if these meals were meant as a 'relish for father' and not as main dishes for the whole family, it's clear that these, whether served with anything else (the book does not actually specify accompanying dishes) or not, were very small and frugal indeed and could hardly have provided enough energy for a man doing any sort of active work.

A bestseller that went into more than twenty editions, *Tried Favourites*, was full of traditionally thrifty recipes, such as:

- White soup: 2oz potatoes, 2 pints water
- Potato bridies: a few boiled and mashed potatoes coated with mince, fried in hot fat
- Plain boiled barley pudding: 1 teacup barley soaked overnight in 3 teacups water, then boiled till soft, and after adding 3 teacups milk boiled for a further 1½ hours
- Economy pudding: 4oz stale breadcrumbs, 6oz chopped suet, 2 eggs, spoonful brown sugar, 2 large tablespoons jam[40]

The Best Way series of books also contained economical recipes, such as:

- Stella pudding: 1½oz butter, ½oz flour, ½ pint milk, sugar to taste, teaspoon of ground ginger, 2 eggs and brown breadcrumbs, the whole steamed for an hour
- Cheese puffs: 3 tablespoons of grated cheese, 2 tablespoons flour, 1 egg and 1oz butter, the whole deep fried
- Bread cutlets: thick slices of bread dipped in milk and egg, sprinkled with salt and pepper, fried in 1 tablespoon dripping[41]

Economical cooking depended on careful pre-planning, with several books offering advice on basic nutrition that would not go amiss today. Recommendations included daily intake of bread and breakfast cereal, fruit, milk (adults 1 pint, children 1-2 pints), meat with a little fat, and vegetables (one cooked, one either raw or as salad) plus twice-weekly allowances of cheese; dried beans, lentils, etc.; macaroni and spaghetti; fish; offal, etc.; and tomatoes. Elizabeth Craig was particularly helpful in this respect, providing shopping lists of groceries and fresh foods. A housewife catering for two adults and one child on a weekly food allowance of 30s might, for example, base her menus around Craig's recommendations of 4lb of fruit, 3lb of green vegetables, 5lb of other vegetables and 7½lb of potatoes, and six loaves of bread. Working on such tiny margins it would have been almost impossible to waste money on what we would nowadays consider as 'treats', and consequently people would have been healthier following such recommendations. In her 1934 book, *Economical Cookery*, Craig also gave seven days' worth of menus for two adults and four children on a food allowance of 35s per week. Here, menus included kedgeree (made with 2oz of rice, 6oz of cooked fish and one hard-boiled egg), fish pie and apple shortcake. A modern equivalent recipe for kedgeree might use 500g/1lb of fish and 100g/4oz of rice: clearly, quantities have increased steadily over the intervening seventy years.

Sometimes a cookery book would supply a recipe and a cheaper alternative. Scotch eggs, for example, could be made in two ways: either with ½lb of sausage meat enclosing the eggs in the traditional way or, more economically, with the eggs sliced, arranged in a star shape and served on a bed of mashed potatoes, peas and breadcrumbs.

Emelie Waller, writing in the mid-1930s, felt that the most important way for a family to achieve good health was by giving give them good, simple food – carefully cooked and providing a basic yet varied diet. Her recipes are definitely simple and they are also extremely thrifty. Scrambled eggs for five made with four eggs and 1 tablespoon of cornflour; butter beans on toast using 8oz of soaked butter beans, two rashers of bacon, an onion, some dripping and flour; and fish pie made with 8oz of fish, three onions and as many potatoes as necessary.[42] Many families struggled through the 'Hungry Thirties' on much less than this very basic yet healthy diet. Even thriftier was Sago Soup: this comprised nothing but 3 pints of good stock and 1½oz of fine sago.[43]

Florence White's classic *Good Things in England* (1932) contained a wide variety of traditional economical dishes, including:

- Brewis: boiling water poured over a crust of bread and then drained off, seasoned with salt and pepper and eaten with a spoon from a breakfast cup
- Champ: potatoes, hot milk, butter, cooked peas, onions, pepper and salt
- Fried cakes: 3oz self-raising flour, milk to make a stiff dough, and fat for frying[44]

Some writers were very forthright about waste, inefficiency and the need for thrift. Elizabeth Craig's 1930s cookery books are full of hints on using up leftovers and planning meals carefully to avoid waste. Armed with one of her books, the housewife could learn many useful skills such as how to do twenty things with a packet of jelly, or cater for a family of three on 30s a week.[45] In her opinion, British housewives were far too careless with cold meat and soup meat (the meat left over from stock making), and she had several suggestions for using it up, including giblet broth, rissoles and croquettes. It could also be diced up and mixed with mayonnaise and mustard to taste or, alternatively, heated up in a curry sauce and served with boiled rice and jacket potatoes. 1lb of soup meat would make a pie with broth, margarine and lemon juice with a breadcrumb topping, and 2lb would make a meat hash with bacon, onions and some broth. The point was that nothing needed to be wasted if you knew what to do with it – a point much in vogue with modern writers of thrifty cookery books.

Another book, also called *Economical Cookery* and with a foreword by *Good Housekeeping's* D.D. Cottington-Taylor, carried the idea of thrifty catering even further. A complete year's menus were provided, with prices given for Sunday's meals (1lb of prunes for 6d, 4lb of veal for 4s). There were also chapters on using up leftovers, and cooking with limited equipment and very little time. None of them seem particularly effective, but were presumably meant as a form of 'emergency cooking', as it was known, to be done when unexpected guests turned up. The recipes included junket, grilled kippers and fruit pancakes. The truly thrifty section of *Economical Cookery* is the chapter entitled 'Sixpenny Dishes', where all manner of cheap recipes could be made for 6*d*:

- Kedgeree: 6oz smoked fillets, 3oz rice, 1 egg, butter, nutmeg
- Savoury rice: 8oz rice, 3oz grated cheese, ½ pint milk, salt and pepper, brown breadcrumbs
- Cheese pudding: 3oz breadcrumbs, 2oz cheese, 1oz margarine, salt and pepper, made mustard, 1 egg, ½ pint milk
- Poor knight's pudding: 3 slices stale bread, 1 egg, 1 teaspoon sugar, 1/8 teaspoon cinnamon, 1/4 pint milk, dripping to fry bread
- Pork and beans: 4oz fat pork or bacon, 8oz haricot or butter beans, 1 onion
- Stuffed sheep's heart: 1 sheep's heart, 2oz breadcrumbs, 1 dessertspoon suet, 1oz dripping, seasonings[46]

Some dishes had names that indicated particularly stringent economy. Recipes such as:

- Half-pay pudding: 4oz each suet, flour, currants, raisins and breadcrumbs, 2 tablespoons treacle, ½ pint milk
- War butter: 1 teaspoon Foster Clark's custard powder, 1/4 pint milk, a little salt, 4oz margarine
- Scrap pie: 3oz dripping, 8oz fine oatmeal (or 4oz each oatmeal and flour), and ½ teaspoon salt made into very short pastry. Layers of leftover meat, potatoes, onions and stock to make pie filling
- Economical soup: 2 onions, 2oz butter, the water in which a cauliflower had previously been boiled, scraps of stale bread, a small amount of milk. [This recipe was said to be an excellent one for use in soup kitchens]
- Economy rissoles: equal quantities of leftover porridge and dry boiled rice, any scraps of cold meat, a small amount of onion, a pinch of herbs, seasoning[47]

Thrifty Meat Recipes

Housewives cooked and used many cuts of meat that are no longer available to the public, such as cows' heels and calves' heads. With some forward planning it was possible to make a variety of dishes for mealtimes and for the store cupboard.

MODERN HINT

Traditional butchers are often much cheaper and are invariably far more knowledgeable about their products than any supermarket.

Brawn and potted meat could be made in advance and kept until needed, both dishes being made with the addition of leftovers. Some thrifty dishes made from these ingredients included:

- Clear mock turtle soup (a calf's head)
- Soup or brawn (a cow heel plus 2 pickled sheep tongues)
- Giblet soup or giblet pie (turkey giblets)
- Kidney soup
- Galantine of veal (lambs' tongues)
- Ox brain fritters
- Russian soup (an ox head, served steamed or roasted)
- Ox liver and onion hotpot, ox liver and parsnips
- Oxtail soup
- Pig's head served roasted with onions and apples
- Baked sheep's head and barley broth (a sheep's head plus trotters)
- Mutton duck (a shoulder of mutton, dripping, onions, breadcrumbs)

Ingredients that could be made into more than one dish were seen as particularly thrifty. Forward planning, as with a cooking morning, was necessary to ensure that nothing was wasted. However, the time saved by cooking a number of meals at once would almost certainly have made up for the minor inconvenience of juggling several different processes. One of the most economical cuts of meat was a leg bone of beef, which cost between 2s and 2s 6d in 1913. Used carefully it would yield four or five meals, including a cold dish served with salad; a casserole with carrots, onions and turnips; a hot dish served with gravy; and soup from the liquor left after the initial boiling. The marrow, removed from the bone at the beginning of the operation, was added to the fat that arose from boiling, and was saved for making cakes and pastry.

Sheep's tongues and green peas – an example of attractive presentation.

Bone marrow was a delicacy enjoyed by Queen Victoria, and was recommended as a pick-me-up for sickly children. In the Georgian period it was made, according to Dorothy Hartley, by breaking the bones, sealing the ends in a pastry case and baking them. The marrow melted and was poured out onto hot buttered toast and eaten with a special long, thin, silver marrow spoon or, as above, saved for pastry making.[48]

Another delicacy, much enjoyed in the author's childhood home, was beef dripping. The juices that dripped from the roasting meat were poured into a large basin and left to cool. It separated into a hard, fat layer on top with a dark, savoury jelly underneath, and was spread on hot toast with a generous scoop of top and bottom layers.

Cold Meat

Recipes for cold meat dishes were popular because they used up oddments and extended the life of scraps that might otherwise have been thrown away. It is debatable how much actual 'saving' went on in the average kitchen, especially when the cost of fuel and the time spent coaxing tiny scraps from mincing machines and brushing crumbs from breadboards into tins is factored in, but history is silent on the matter. It may simply have been taken for granted that nothing was squandered if a possible use could be found for it. In households where every penny was turned over twice before it was spent, such economy may have made the difference between penury and comfort. Cold meat recipes included:

- Scotch dainty-bit: a large potato stuffed with minced meat
- Macaroni mould: cold mince and macaroni served with white sauce
- Sea pie: cold meat layered in a pie dish with sliced potatoes, ·carrots and onions
- Beef porcupine: cold beef minced and made into a stiff paste with mashed potatoes and beaten egg, shaped into a roll with rolled-up strips of bacon pushed into it to resemble a porcupine[49]

Patriotic Recipes

Recipes were altered and renamed according to the politics of the day, the economic climate and many other subtle crosscurrents that we can only guess at today. Among the thrifty recipes with wartime associations or patriotic names that appeared in post-First World War cookery books were:

- British pie: made with hard-boiled eggs, onion, tomatoes, sliced beetroot, and potatoes layered in a dish and covered with mashed potatoes.
- Canadian war cake: contained no fat, eggs or milk. Made with brown sugar, raisins, mixed spice and salt boiled up then left to cool, then flour and bicarbonate of soda was added plus a little hot water.
- Half-pay pudding (see p50)
- Patriotic pudding: made with butter, sugar, flour, an egg, milk, baking powder and a little jam, the whole steamed for an hour.
- Victory cake: made with flour, margarine, sugar, grated nutmeg, milk, bicarbonate of soda, treacle and mixed fruit.
- War butter (see p50)
- War time buns: a combination of flour and maize flour, margarine, sugar, desiccated coconut, baking powder, a little milk and an egg.
- War time macaroons: made with Quaker oats, margarine and sugar. [50]
- Ladysmith pudding: stale bread boiled in milk until thick, then butter, sugar, cocoa and vanilla essence added, with the yolks then whites of three eggs.
- Nelson's patriotic cream: 1oz of unsweetened chocolate melted in a pint of cream with a packet of Nelson's Vanilla

Cream added. The whites of three eggs whisked in, a half pint of Nelson's Concentrated Port-Wine Jelly dissolved in boiling water with some of it poured into an ornamental mould. The cream mixture was poured in and it was left to set. The recipe says that it was 'designed to show the khaki colours'[51]

Feeding Invalids

According to old cookery books, the point of invalid cookery was to restore the patient's jaded appetite by coaxing them to eat specially-prepared meals that would nourish and stimulate without putting any strain on the digestive system. This meant that a lot of the food prepared for invalids was simple, somewhat bland and, especially with recipes from the early part of the century, had most of the nourishment cooked out of it before it even reached the patient. Beef tea, toast water, gruel, bread-and-milk and arrowroot pudding were all recommended, as was baked flour, which was said to be good for cases of phthisis (TB) and various conditions known as 'wasting diseases'. Catering for an invalid diet might well have put a considerable strain on a small budget, especially if special ingredients had to be bought. Some recipes seem to be less worth the making than others, particularly meat-based dishes depending on several hours cooking, such as:

- Slowly made beef tea: lean beef cut small and steeped in water for 12 hours, then stewed slowly for 3 hours and strained and pressed through a strainer
- Chicken broth: a chicken boiled for 2 hours
- Invalid jelly: 8oz each veal, mutton and steak, steamed for 6 hours[52]

Fish dishes, quickly cooked, were more nutritious than those based around meat:

- Fish cooked in paper: dipped in seasoned flour and baked in a paper bag for about 15 minutes
- Steamed plaice: steamed for 5 minutes between 2 buttered plates

Sweet dishes often included milk puddings, made with or without eggs. Jellies were also popular: an egg jelly (2 lemons, 2 eggs, 2oz of sugar, ½oz of gelatine and ½ pint of water) cost approximately 4*d* in 1914. Jellies were not particularly nourishing but they could be made in a variety of colours and shapes using pretty moulds, and for this reason they were frequently included in invalid cookery. Vegetables were less popular: green vegetables such as cauliflower and asparagus were the first choice if they could be afforded, but root vegetables were usually avoided as they were held to be difficult to digest – probably partly because they were usually overcooked.

Some recipes for invalid cookery may seem particularly strange to modern eyes:

- Baked flour: 1lb flour tied up tightly into a pudding cloth and boiled for 4 hours. A hard shell would form as the flour baked and this was cut away and the inside was reduced to powder with a grater. 1 tablespoon of the powder was added to 1 tablespoon cold milk and mixed with 1 pint boiling milk [this, goodness knows why, was held to be good for delicate children and TB cases]
- Artificial asses' milk: 4 sheep's trotters simmered 20 minutes in 1 pint milk until reduced to ½ pint. ½oz sugar and 1 pint milk were

Tray for an invalid, 1914.

Soup cup for an invalid, 1914.

then added [excellent, stated the recipe, for patients suffering from wasting diseases]

- Toast water (also known as breadberry water or brewis): 1 slice of toast broken into a large cup of boiling water, cooled and strained
- Albumenised egg: 1 raw egg broken into a basin of cold water and left to soak for 12 hours. Strain water off and poach [The recipe stated that the result 'will taste very brittle and melt in the mouth']⁵³

Cooking for Diabetics

Cooking for diabetics was seen as a particular challenge in the 1910s. *Home Cookery & Comforts* referred to diabetes as 'a nervous disorder' and 'a dreaded ailment', and attributed it to the rush of modern life.⁵⁴ Readymade foods were very expensive, but homemade diabetic food was seen as just as good and also said to be ideal for people wishing to lose weight. Starch and sugar were to be avoided, and ground nuts, prepared bran, almond meal and a proprietary food called Plasmon took the place of flour, gravy and soup thickeners. Saccharine was recommended instead of sugar and fruit was to be avoided except for lemons and Seville oranges. The diabetic could look forward to dishes such as:

- Diabetic bread (made with almond meal and bran)
- Stewed mushrooms with almond sauce
- Watercress cream
- Gluten omelette
- Almond cream dessert⁵⁵

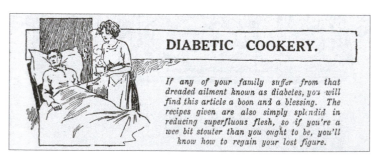

DIABETIC COOKERY.

If any of your family suffer from that dreaded ailment known as diabetes, you will find this article a boon and a blessing. The recipes given are also simply splendid in reducing superfluous flesh, so if you're a wee bit stouter than you ought to be, you'll know how to regain your lost figure.

Diabetes, 1913.

Feeding Elderly People

Many households were composed of several generations, with elderly parents living with their children and grandchildren. Feeding elderly people was therefore often part of everyday cooking, although it was recommended that they ate different food to the rest of the family where possible. Families who could afford to do this could follow recipes given in *Tried Favourites* and *Home Cookery & Comforts*.

According to these books, food for the elderly should be light, nourishing and digestible, and served attractively to tempt the appetite – 'special daintiness should mark the tray put before an old person'.[56] All food should be 'plain', i.e. no rich sauces to irritate a supposedly enfeebled digestive system, and nothing fried or fatty. Fish was thought to be too stimulating unless served plain and boiled, fancy puddings were to be avoided and cake, if allowed, was to be of a plain variety only.

As plain nutritious cooking was recommended by nearly all thrifty cookery books, it would probably not have been too difficult to cater for an elderly relative. *Home Cookery & Comforts* advised a bit of forward thinking – buying, for example, a small casserole in which a beef oyster or a chop could be cooked. Other meals might comprise a small helping of cabbage that could be pressed into a teacup and unmoulded as a small individual helping, or a small syrup pudding quickly made for Saturday dinner when the rest of the family was having boiled plum duff with currants. An individual cornflour mould (1oz cornflour, ½ pint of milk, stewed fruit, sugar to taste) was simple to make as the fruit could be conveniently diverted from the family's fruit tart, and a milk jelly could be made while a rice pudding was prepared. This is another example of the basic frugal skill of overlapping recipes, saving fuel and making multiple dishes from a common ingredient.

Feeding Children

Many thousands of working-class children in the early twentieth century lived on the most basic diet of tea with condensed milk, bread with margarine or treacle, with perhaps an occasional taste of meat. Street food such as pies, fish and chips or baked potatoes were available to those who could afford them, but many children went hungry or suffered from malnutrition-linked diseases such as rickets.

In many cities soup kitchens run by churches and organisations such as the Salvation Army offered a basic farthing breakfast (a mug of cocoa and two slices of bread and jam for example) and some bakeries would sell bags of stale cake and biscuits. Many houses had inadequate cooking facilities – some had none at all – and many families lived in the most abject poverty. However, many housewives were adept at producing wholesome meals with the minimum of facilities, feeding their families on huge rice puddings, bread puddings, and 'cauldrons' full of soup or rabbit stew.

Food prepared specifically for children was only possible when there was a little extra money to go round. Children were rarely consulted on likes and dislikes, but were expected to eat what was put before them; often the alternative was seeing the uneaten food put before them again at the next meal, and some meals did not adapt happily to this treatment. Some foods were seen as unsuitable, even unsafe, for children, whose digestive systems were thought to be delicate and in need of the blandest diet procurable. *Tried Favourites* included this list of 'forbidden' foodstuffs:

- Meat: ham, sausages, pork, corned beef, goose, duck, game, kidneys, liver, bacon, meat stews and fried meat
- Fish: salt fish
- Vegetables: raw cucumbers and tomatoes were 'specially objectionable'. 'Nearly as bad' were cabbage, raw onions and baked or fried potatoes[57]
- Fruit: all stale fruit, all out of season fruit
- Bread and cakes: all new bread, hot buttered toast or scones and sweet, rich or iced cakes
- Desserts: pastry, tarts, dried fruit and all sweets
- Drinks: tea, coffee, wine, beer, cider and soda water

Most books advised against cream or any rich foods whatsoever. A child raised the *Tried Favourites* way would have been allowed to eat these foods:

- Oatmeal porridge (well-boiled)
- A quart of milk a day made into bread and milk, custards, milk pudding, etc.
- Suet pudding
- Mashed potatoes, green peas (mashed up), finely cut French beans
- Eggs (lightly boiled, poached or scrambled)

- Beef (roasted or boiled), mutton, fish, poultry, soups and broths
- Wheaten bread
- Ripe fruit in season
- Homemade jam
- Water or weak cocoa to drink

Foods such as these were probably not calculated to make food interesting or exciting to children in any way. The only times that a slightly more exciting diet came their way was birthdays and Christmas time – party food was much richer than everyday fare and bilious attacks and upset stomachs doubtless reinforced the view that rich food was clearly not good for children. As an example of culinary extravagance, it must be hard to top the recipe for a party delicacy given in a 1909 household manual for a jelly made with flakes of pure gold leaf.[58]

One way to hoodwink children into eating was to give boring or everyday food an exciting name, such as:

- Wendy salad: lettuce, tomato, watercress, beetroot and a little cream cheese
- Sunshine eggs: eggs steamed in jellied stock made sunshine colour by the addition of a touch of saffron
- Brigade pudding: suet crust filled with currants, mixed peel and golden syrup
- Mickey Mouse salad: bananas, cherries, red currants, orange and lemon juice
- Red Riding Hood pudding: rhubarb and sponge cake covered with raspberry jelly[59]

Finally, a cold sweet that children probably never tasted was the unlikely sounding chipolata trifle. Although its name conjures up all sorts of food nightmares, it was simply a combination of sponge cakes moistened with sherry and lemon juice, spread with jam, covered with custard and then topped with ratafia biscuits, cream and cherries.[60]

Christmas

Christmas cooking was taken very seriously. Housewives would often put money aside for buying the fruit and flour for cakes and puddings, and preparations usually started towards the end of October when the new consignment of dried fruit appeared in the shops. Forward thinking and advance preparation meant that, in the words of one magazine, 'the extra work entailed by the Christmas festivities loses its terror'.[61] Most housewives made puddings, a cake and mincemeat in advance, and made a special dinner on Christmas Day. Extras such as suet and breadcrumbs were prepared and stored, and by November the organised housewife could look with satisfaction at the contents of her store cupboard. Christmas puddings had been available in shops since the Boer War, but many housewives preferred to make their own from scratch.

Thrifty recipes abounded. Christmas puddings could be made without eggs; without sugar, eggs and milk; or without suet. The following dish does not contain sugar, eggs or milk, and its unusual combination of ingredients is a deliberate attempt to make a little go a long way. For example, carrots provide sweetness and a certain unusual flavour and texture, and mashed potatoes and breadcrumbs add bulk to what would otherwise be a very dull, stodgy recipe:

- 4oz each flour, suet, raw grated carrot, mashed potatoes and stoned dates; 2oz breadcrumbs; 3oz currants; 1oz candied peel; nutmeg; a pinch of salt

A really cheap, small Christmas pudding:

- 1 pint breadcrumbs soaked in hot water; 1 teacup each golden syrup and raisins; 1 teaspoon allspice; ½ teaspoon ground ginger; 1 breakfast cup self-raising flour; ½ teaspoon bicarbonate of soda; 1 dessertspoon nut butter.
- A cheap pouring sauce was made from 1 teacup golden syrup, ½ teacup water and the grated rind and juice of a lemon[62]

A hard-times Christmas cake:

- 8oz margarine, 2½ cups milk, 8oz treacle, 12oz stoned raisins, 1 teaspoon mixed spice, 8oz Demerara sugar, 2 teaspoons baking soda, 1½lb flour, 2oz candied peel, 8oz cleaned currants[63]

MODERN HINT

Christmas cooking always makes the house smell festive. Involve children as soon as they can hold a wooden spoon: they can cut out pastry for mince pies, stir the cake mixture, make marzipan animals, pop the skins off the almonds and decorate the cake – don't forget to take photos of their creations.

Mock Food

Nicola Humble has pointed out that there are two ways to present mock, or imitation, food: it can either look approximately right or it can taste approximately right. During the Second World War, it was more important to get the appearance right, but during and after the First World War the taste was the important factor. There are many ingenious mock foods, prepared by substituting a cheaper or more available ingredient, or using something completely different to get the desired result. Eleanour Sinclair Rohde's 1939 *Haybox Cookery Book* included mock hare soup using gravy beef, mock goose using breast of mutton, and mock venison using cold mutton, redcurrant jelly and mushroom ketchup. Another book included recipes for mock fish (made from parsnips), mock goose (made from vegetable marrow), and mock steak (made from haricot beans).[64] Turkey, duck or goose were all popular choices for Christmas dinner in the 1930s, but if funds did not run to this expense the thrifty housewife could often find a substitute. Other festive mock foods included:

- Cottage goose: 3lb unsalted streaky pork, 1lb sausages, three onions, 4oz breadcrumbs, sage, milk to bind. The sausages were skinned and laid on the pork, a sage and onion stuffing was spread over, the pork was rolled up and sewn, scored, and baked for 2 hours
- Poor man's goose: Sliced apples sprinkled with sugar, layered with sage and onion stuffing, slices of liver, sliced salted potatoes, dotted with dripping and baked for 1 hour. 'Try this dish when you want a cheap dinner, and if you shut your eyes you will think you are eating real goose with apple sauce and sage and onion stuffing'[65]
- Mock pork: 8oz haricot beans soaked overnight, simmered with 2 finely chopped onions and mashed with 2oz margarine, 4oz

breadcrumbs, 1 tablespoon sage, bound with 1 egg and ½ teacup of milk. Form into a thick roll and bake till brown, basting as needed. Serve with apple sauce

Avoiding Waste

'In a well-managed household, nothing need be wasted'.[66] This comment was echoed for many years by writers on domestic matters, whether their books were aimed at the affluent or the far less so.

Traditionally servants were blamed for waste in the kitchen. Their indifference and lack of knowledge of basic cookery was seen as the reason for their legendary and lavish hand with cream, eggs and butter, and for throwing away perfectly good vegetable water and oddments of bread, both of which could be used to good account.

However, housewives doing their own cooking had no such excuses, and those who had to watch the pennies had to be especially careful not to waste anything. Thrifty cookery books were full of advice on avoiding waste, and many of them provided ingenious ways for using up bits and pieces that would otherwise have been discarded. Some examples:

- Meat liquor: made a good foundation for soup
- Meat trimmings and bones: stock
- Shank bones (ham): stock for pea soup
- Shank bones (mutton): soups and gravies
- Bone marrow: carefully extracted by heating, this was an old-fashioned delicacy
- Small oddments of meat: potted meat
- Fish liquor: replaced the milk or water in the sauce served with the fish
- Fish bones and skin: made soup or stock base (those with a bent for handicrafts could also use the fish bones to make various decorative items for the home)
- Poultry carcasses and giblets: stock, soup, or giblet pie
- Breadcrumbs, crusts and leftover slices: puddings, gratin toppings, coating for rissoles, boiled ham or fish dishes (it was considered bad form to serve bread that had already been sliced for one meal at another meal)
- Cake crumbs and leftover biscuits: embellished with cream, custard, jam or fruit and transformed into any of the 'little dishes' or 'dainty dishes' so popular in cookery books of the period –

some of these were so dainty that the term could almost be seen as a euphemism for not having enough to eat

- Potato and orange peelings: dried and used as firelighters
- Orange pips: soaked in water and stored, their high pectin content making them a useful addition to homemade marmalade
- Fruit stones: dried and put in a paper bag, good for perking up a dying fire
- Lemon husks: used for polishing the Benares brassware that was so popular between the wars
- Celery: the tough, stringy parts were scraped off, blanched and added to soup
- Fat: rendered and clarified for reuse

MODERN HINT

Compost bins and freezers make light work of leftovers.

The Stockpot

There were several varieties of stock – brown, white, game, vegetable and fish – and several ways of making it – first, second, bone, vegetable, general, pot liquor, and glaze. Beef or mutton made brown stock, chicken or veal made white stock, and fish bones and trimmings made fish stock; these in turn formed the basis of many different varieties of soup, such as cream soup (veal bones) or kidney soup (mutton bones). Provided the basic rules were followed, the process of making stock was simple. Bones were stripped of marrow and chopped into small pieces, any adhering meat was chopped up and any fat was removed. The bones were put into cold water if the meat was fresh, hot water for cooked meat, and left for six hours, after which the water was heated slowly to boiling point. Any froth was skimmed off with a slotted spoon and the stock was left to simmer for another six or seven hours, with any seasonings and vegetables

Stockpot, 1910s.

added one hour before the end of cooking. The cake of fat that formed on the surface during boiling and simmering was removed and set aside to be clarified for later frying or baking. The stock was strained off for use, the bones were put aside for reuse, and the pot was washed and left to air until the next day when the whole process was started again with fresh ingredients. Alternatively, the process could last a week, with successive re-boilings as fresh ingredients were added.

Whether or not the finished product retained any nutritional value after such treatment is debatable, but the contents of the stockpot provided the basis for dozens of economical recipes. These included Delhi broth (3*d* worth of bones, 4 leeks, salt and pepper), bread soup (2 slices stale bread, 1 pint of hot milk, 1 onion, 1oz of butter and seasoning), and cow heel broth (1 cow heel, peppercorns, thyme and parsley).

Leftovers

Most cookery books covered the subject of leftovers in some detail. One exception was *Dinners for Beginners* by Rachel and Margaret Ryan. They were of the unusual opinion (for their time) that the economies bought by using up leftovers in the next day's meals were not particularly helpful, especially in the small household of one or two people. They instead suggested arranging meals so that the problem did not arise because nothing was left over in the first place.

Although their book deals with amateur cooks catering for small dinner parties without help and in tiny kitchens, their advice also applied to everyday meal planning: many women cooked in tiny, chaotic kitchens and found it difficult to get everything prepared and dished up in an organised way. Working to a timetable – as with a cooking morning – involved forward planning and ensured, for example, that pastry oddments were collected and made into jam tarts straightaway, rather than left in a damp heap 'for later'. Other writers were generally not of this opinion, and cookery and housekeeping advice books were full of hints and recipes for what was sometimes called *rechauffé* cookery – more usually known as using up leftovers. Odds and ends that could be used up included:

- ● Remnants of a meat pie and a mutton bone: croquettes, rissoles, fritters or a curry

- Beef bones with meat attached: devilled and grilled dishes
- Lamb scraps: 1 breakfast cup of lamb scraps and 1 of cooked macaroni. A cup of milk with two beaten eggs poured over the lamb and macaroni
- Cold potatoes: fried or shaped into croquettes
- Fish pieces: egg-and-breadcrumbed and fried for breakfast; or kedgeree
- Tiny scraps of meat or fish: mixed with tomato sauce or gravy and spread on hot buttered toast
- Green vegetables: bubble and squeak; or added to soup
- Ham bone: the scraps potted and the bone added to the stockpot

Throwing away leftovers (also called scraps or pieces) was not only wasteful and unthrifty; during the First World War it had also been unpatriotic and a criminal offence during a time when food was scarce (see Chapter Five). It was universally agreed that an efficient housewife made use of all the leftovers. Everything, it seems, could be made into something else. For example, there were dozens of ideas for ways to use up oddments of bread, whether crumbs from the breadboard, crusts from the cut loaf, or slices from the dinner table. Some examples were:

- Converting any oddments into crumbs for gratins, rissoles or croquettes; adding to bread sauce; making rasping or croutons; eking out minced meat or suet puddings
- Slices: key ingredients in many puddings (bread, hospitality, Valencia, Betty's, summer, Swiss, Free Kirk and golden) and apple charlotte

One way to make breadcrumbs was to rub the bread through a wire cake stand or cooling rack. Anyone who has tried this (or saves breadcrumbs from the breadboard) will agree that it is a very long-winded way to create or collect crumbs!

MODERN HINT

Breadcrumbs seem to breed exponentially, so it's worth keeping a decent-sized plastic box in the freezer and adding crumbs as they accumulate.

Fish remnants could be made into fishcakes, patties, cutlets, soufflés, kedgeree, fish mould, gratins, and curries. Even an unpromising collection of oddments such as a bloater, some boiled rice, cold cooked potatoes, some cooked haricot beans, stock, 2 tomatoes and a few bacon rinds could, with a few additions, turn up at the table next day as an appetising meal.

Leftover meat could be utilised in several ways:

- Small scraps could be minced or added to bubble and squeak or rissoles
- Fat and soup or stock skimmings could be clarified for dripping, or fat for frying
- Scraps of bacon rind flavoured soup and even the water used to boil hams could be used for soup stock

Meat could also be devilled, scalloped, casseroled or curried and, if the pieces were really too small to be reused at all they could be pounded smooth, seasoned and potted, or made into galantine.

The dessert course benefited hugely from the addition of leftovers:

- Stale cake: trifles, cabinet pudding, queen's pudding
- Sweet pastry scraps: cheese straws, jam tarts, sandwiched with jam or whipped cream, cream horns
- Sago: maids of honour
- An uneaten half of a fruit tart could be transformed by removing the fruit to a cut-glass dish (fruit was always nicer to look at when it was served in glass dishes), cutting the pastry into neat pieces and serving it with whipped cream

Suppertime was often seen as the best meal for slipping in leftovers. Dishes might include potted ham (using the meat left on a ham bone); brown twins (using slices of brown bread), batter and bacon (a slice of cold boiled bacon or two rashers); or Brussels sprout fritters. One book referred to supper as a meal where the housewife was not required to spend hours at the stove, hinting that small, savoury type meals were by far the best thing to serve at supper. If leftovers could be used, all the better.

Even melted ice-cream (popular in America but, because of ice making problems, less used in the UK at this time) came into its own. The melted and runny remains from the table could be used in cakes (omitting the milk and reducing the fat and sugar in the recipe);

made into a cold dessert (adding gelatine and stirring in chopped marshmallows); or it could be added to cookies.

Cooking Mornings/Whole Dinner Menus

By the 1920s women were becoming resigned to the necessity of doing their own cooking and many basic cookery books were appearing on the market, aimed at servant-less households where the mistress of the house had minimal knowledge of cookery techniques. In addition, some households had a kitchen full of redundant *batterie de cuisine* whose mysteries were known only to the departed cook, and often the kitchens themselves were not particularly attractive or convenient to work in. Such problems were widespread as few houses were built with convenient kitchen quarters before the 1930s.

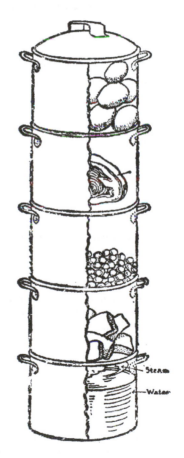

Cooking mornings were seen as the best way to save time and money. Mrs Peel's *Daily Mail Cookbook* gave detailed instructions for a cooking morning that would produce a week's worth of dishes in one burst of energy. The most important part of such activity was preparation, essential when nearly every activity had to be carefully organised and dovetailed into the overall process. First, the range had to be primed and ready with clean flues and a good 'draw'. Cooking mornings seem to be one of the few times where a range had the edge over a gas stove. Its steady heat was suitable for a variety of dishes and its greater area and

Steamer, 1920s.

versatile inner space could cook several things at once: contemporary gas stoves were small and did not have the same facilities as a range. Next, all ingredients had to be prepared. Dried fruit was picked over to remove grit, stones and pips, and then cleaned – a sticky and tedious job in itself before ready-to-use varieties were available. After that, all equipment had to be clean and ready, and sufficient water had to be heated, both for cooking and for the piles of washing-up that inevitably followed a cooking morning. If a gas oven was used, it might take 20 minutes to reach its required temperature: the gas was then turned down until the oven was ready for use. At last, the cooking morning could begin. From then on, the housewife had to move with some degree of speed and efficiency, overlapping processes to ensure that every dish went into the oven or steamer at just the right moment to take maximum advantage of the heat without wasting fuel, water or time. The following dishes could be prepared in a gas oven or on a range, and would last a family of six for four or five days:

- In the oven: pastry, cakes, scones, baked joints, baked potatoes, vegetable or rabbit casserole, pot roast, baked puddings, baked fish, baked soufflé
- On the fire and hot plate in a two- or three-tier steamer: suet puddings, potatoes, steamed soufflé, vegetables
- On the hot plates: sauces, blancmanges, custards, stewed fruit, jellies, stock, soup; fat could also be rendered at this point

The order in which the various dishes were cooked was important. Milk puddings went on the top shelf to start cooking while the oven was heating up for small cakes, scones and pastry. The milk puddings could be removed when the heat was right and another dish took their place; they could be put back in the oven as and when space permitted. Meat and large cakes went in after small cakes and pastry (the first 15 minutes in a hot oven and then moved to a cooler part to continue cooking); soup, etc., was made while the meat was cooking. This system of overlapping saved fuel and time, and is still useful today.

Cooking mornings were also handy for doubling-up a range of dishes by overlapping ingredients, thus saving time and fuel later in the week. For example, rather than prepare potatoes three times for three separate meals, the thrifty housewife was encouraged to parboil a triple quantity on Saturday and keep the surplus until needed. If she was making pastry, she might as well make a few apple turnovers as well, thus saving herself the chore of washing the pastry board, rolling pin, pastry brush, knife and basin twice over.

However, as the majority of cooking was done from scratch with raw materials, everything took much longer than today. A shepherd's pie, for example, was not simply a matter of first thawing a pack of supermarket mince; leftover meat was carefully kept aside until enough was ready for putting through the mincer. Alternatively, one 1920s recipe began with instructions for boiling a sheep's head, then boning it and cutting it into pieces. According to another recipe, boiling a sheep's head involved splitting the head, removing the brains, washing the head and removing any bone splinters, then soaking it in salt water for an hour. After this the head was boiled up in fresh water with herbs and seasoning, then skimmed and cooked for anything up to 3 hours. The brains, washed and put into cold salt water on removal from the head, were skinned, boiled in the liquor in which the head was cooked and then fried in seasoned flour. Only then could the process of removing the meat from the bones actually begin, and only after that could it be put through the mincing machine and the rest of the recipe completed.

If the thought of a cooking morning was more than the housewife could bear, she could follow the advice given in cookery books written specifically for users of gas stoves. This was the simpler method of preparing a complete menu to be cooked at the same heat for the same time, a system that is still encouraged today as it saves time, conserves energy and fills up the oven usefully. Menus included:

- Roast beef and potatoes, Yorkshire pudding; apricot charlotte (Regulo 7; 1 hour)
- Braised loin of mutton, baked potatoes; rice pudding, stewed prunes (Regulo 4; 1 hour 45 minutes)
- Veal and ham pie, potato and tomato casserole; date pudding (Regulo 4; 2 hours)

MODERN HINT

Cooking mornings are still worth the effort. Keep a list of current favourite cake or cookie recipes, or top up the freezer with lasagne or fish pie — perfect for mealtimes when inspiration refuses to strike and time is short.

Economical Use of Ovens and Fuel

Oven temperature was a tricky business before the advent of automatic and standardised temperature control. Cookery books generally included descriptions such as 'hot', 'moderate' or 'slow', or suggested that the housewife put her hand in the oven to see how hot it was. This tried-and-tested idea was fine for the experienced cook, but there was a less painful test if the housewife wanted to save herself and her fingers from burns. A sheet of white cooking paper was put in the oven for 3 minutes and whatever colour it turned determined the temperature. Yellow meant a slow oven; yellowish-brown a moderate oven; cigar brown a quick oven; chocolate brown a hot oven; and if the paper burned to ashes the oven – probably to no one's surprise – was too hot to use.

From 1923 innovations such as the 'Regulo' on the new 'Radiation' gas ovens meant that cooking was slowly becoming a standardised operation – in stark contrast to the paper burning techniques described above. The 'Regulo' controlled the temperature inside the oven, allowing the housewife to set it to the number indicated in her recipe (a comprehensive cookery book was supplied with each 'Radiation' oven). Its main advantages were that the interior temperature was consistent, the stove, once set, needed little further attention until the cooking was finished, and a dish could be replicated in full confidence that it would turn out the same over and over again.

The Radiation Company, manufacturer of the hugely popular 'New World' gas oven, claimed to be the first to introduce an oven with heat control (Modern history has bequeathed to us a completely different meaning to the term 'radiation', which in the 1920s referred simply to the properties of radiated heat). Although many cookery books continued to use the familiar 'hot', 'moderate', or 'slow' directions, other firms followed suit so that one truly democratic cookery book written in the 1930s included five different oven settings per recipe. They were:

Regulo 2 = Mainstat B	= Ajusto 1-2	= Flavel's Thermostat C (or D)	= Autimo 2 (or 3-4)
Regulo 3 = Mainstat B-C	= Ajusto 2	= Flavels' Thermostat E	= Autimo 4
Regulo 4 = Mainstat C	= Ajusto 3	= Flavel's Thermostat F	= Autimo 5
Regulo 5 = Mainstat D	= Ajusto 4	= Flavel's Thermostat G	= Autimo 6
Regulo 6 = Mainstat D	= Ajusto 4	= Flavel's Thermostat G	= Autimo 6
Regulo 7 = Mainstat E	= Ajusto 5	= Flavel's Thermostat H	= Autimo 7

This battle was not easily won, and evidence can be seen in various cookery books written as late as the 1950s. Nell Heaton's *Complete Cook* included a chart of comparative settings for the same five manufacturers, although their settings had changed completely over the intervening decades, Regulo 6, for example, being equivalent to Flavel H-I, Main E-F, Autimo 7 and Ajusto (or Adjusto) 7. Fortunately for housewifely sanity, Heaton also included definitions of 'slow', 'moderate' and 'hot', with comparative Fahrenheit temperatures.

Hints on fuel saving were legion. The housewife using a gas oven could combine cleaning with fuel economy by washing all the burner rings and jets in the water left over from washing day (or in caustic soda dissolved in boiling water) and regularly poking out any obstructions in the burner holes with a piece of wire. Other ways to economise on gas were:

- Lay an old tin tray over a gas burner to 'spread' the heat to several pans at once
- Put several jars in a large fish kettle or pan of water and cook them all on one burner (or use a multi-tier steamer or sectional pans)
- Never boil a large kettle when a smaller one will do
- Do several days' baking at once, or have regular cooking mornings, loading the oven as carefully as possible to ensure it's used to its maximum capacity
- Avoid heavy iron pans, they take too long to heat up
- Slice vegetables such as carrots; smaller pieces cook faster. Small cakes cook faster than large ones
- Use square or half-moon shaped pans: two used together over one burner used less fuel than two used separately over two burners (something else could cook on the spare burner).
- Prevent the flame from flaring up the sides of a pan; this was said to waste heat
- To prevent this, use a pan that fits the burner rather than one that's too small
- Light the oven between 5 and 15 minutes before using: this gave the heat time to 'settle' after which it could be adjusted to the correct temperature.
- Use a hay box to supplement a gas stove where possible
- Decide on the amount of gas to be allowed for cooking every week, check the meter regularly and keep a note in a small book.

The British Commercial Gas Association (BCGA) *Cooking by Gas* book made life easier for housewives in the early 1920s by giving suggestions for dishes that could be cooked on the hot plate (porridge, water for tea and coffee, boiling milk, fried bacon and bread, six eggs, toast, and the water to wash it all up with) and even gave a breakdown of the amount of gas used – in this case, 11,000BthU/22cu. ft. It pointed out that 1 therm of gas would cook nine such breakfasts.

Housewives using electric ovens could take advantage of the 'whole dinner' idea and cook a roast, potatoes, Yorkshire pudding, baked tomatoes, apple charlotte and cheese straws in the oven all at once. Alternatively, a multi-tiered steamer on the hot plate might contain a beef roll (at the bottom), a steamed jam pudding (in the middle), and vegetables at the top. Water or milk could be heated using the hotplate's residual heat. The trick was to make use of the heat before it died down. Electric ovens were easy to keep clean and required only a daily wipe over with a cloth. They too were recommended for use with a hay box (see below).

Many households used oil stoves. They were popular because they were portable and could replace or supplement a range in summer or if a bout of particularly heavy cooking was imminent, such as for a wedding. They were said to be economical in use as long as the wicks were kept well trimmed, but could smoke in a disagreeable way.

The other standard method of cooking was the coal range. Their main disadvantage seems to have been the inordinate amount of labour spent keeping them clean (raking out flues, hauling coal, regular applications of black lead and burnishing with emery, constant removal of smut and soot from pans, walls, ceiling and windows). They were, however, very useful for odd jobs such as drying wood overnight, burning kitchen refuse and keeping the kitchen warm, and were the best source of heat for cooking mornings.

Hay box Cookery

Any cooking method that saved on fuel was seen as a good thing. With the increases in the price of firewood during the First World War, many families stopped buying bundles of sticks to light fires and began regular stick-scavenging drives. Coal was scarce and people had to find alternative methods of cooking and heating. Fuel-saving ideas included hay boxes, jam jars, paper bags, casseroles, steamers, and chafing dishes.

Of these, the hay box (also known as a hot box, cooking box, or Norwegian box) is the most well known, partly perhaps because of its widespread use during the Second World War; they were also said to have been used by the British Army during the First World War. Its many benefits were described by the National Food Economy League and the Patriotic Food League during the First World War, and later by Judith Silburn in the 1920s, and Elizabeth Craig and Eleanour Sinclair Rohde in the 1930s. The hay box also had a starring part in a children's book published in the 1930s, *The Children who Lived in a Barn*. This is the story of traditional survival skills taught to a family of middle-class children left to cope on their own, and includes a lot of detail about hay boxes and what can be cooked in them. A farmer's wife teaches Sue, the eldest girl, how to cook economical meals in the hay box, and Sue, faced with cooking for her permanently hungry brothers and sisters, quickly discovers that forward thinking is essential to success. Porridge must be 'started off' by preheating before being transferred to the hay box, and bits of porridge had an annoying habit of getting into everything unless lids were firmly on and pans stood upright in the hay.

The hay box was said to be ideal for dishes requiring long, slow cooking such as milk puddings, soups, stews, hotpot or Irish stew, and as it could be left to its own devices it was a boon for the busy housewife. Food would not burn, boil over or dry out, and as it used no gas it saved on fuel. The hay cost 6*d* in the 1920s and the box was easy to come by, most usually a 6*d* wooden Tate sugar box with a lid (if a box was not available a bucket could be used instead). Some books recommended raising the box off the ground on legs to allow for maximum circulation of air. Thick layers of newspaper, secured with tintacks, were used to line the inside of the box and lid, and the interior was then packed with dry, clean hay at least 6in deep. If crumpled-up balls of newspaper, tightly packed, were used instead then the box was known as a 'fireless cooker'. The container to be used was pressed into the hay until a dent was formed, and the lid was secured either with a hasp and staple or with a weight placed on top of it.

A small box with space for one pan was the most convenient size for a one-person household, but larger boxes, suitable for two or three pans or casseroles, were the best size for families. The most suitable containers were earthenware casseroles or aluminium pans (aluminium was light and a good conductor of heat). The pans also had short, 'ear-shaped' handles, as long ones took up too much space. In summer, the hay box could double as an insulated container to store ice or cold food, and if it had been carefully built it could also double as an extra work surface. Scrubbing burnt-on patches from pans and cake tins was a regular and unpleasant job before non-stick pans appeared on the market. If the pan was boiled up with soda and water and then put in the hay box overnight, they would be as good as new in the morning. Mash for chickens would stay hot overnight, water for shaving or washing would be hot when it was needed, tea could be kept hot indefinitely, fruit or tea stains would disappear after a quick boil in borax and an overnight soak – there were endless ways of using a hay box.

However, the hay box had some disadvantages. Prolonged cooking destroyed vitamin content while sparks adhering to a pan transferred straight from the fire could ignite the whole box. Its size made it inconvenient: a wooden box 2ft by 18in could take up a lot of space in a small kitchen. It may have been handy as an extra work surface, although this seems very unlikely as it was far too low to be useful. Silburn suggested covering it with chintz if it was to be kept in the sitting room. Despite all the drawbacks, domestic writers were enthusiastic about what appears almost as a magic box that would cook almost anything, and there were many recipes available. Eleanour Sinclair Rohde's 1939 book included some classic thrifty recipes such as green pea soup, stewed oxtail and frumenty, as well as marmalade, sugar-beet jam and damson cheese. Ms Rohde also sold sugar beet seeds for 6d per packet and said that sugar beet made delicious soup. Some of her recipes are perhaps more a product of her time than of ours, such as her method of making marrow lemon cheese using a 2lb vegetable marrow, a lemon, 12oz of sugar and 3oz of margarine.

Hay box cooking allowed housewives to make use of cheap cuts of meat that needed long, slow cooking, such as shin of beef, and parts of animals such as ox palate and oxtail. Rohde's recipe for boiled sheep's head was a particularly long-winded process involving soaking the head overnight before boiling it for 1 hour and transferring it to the hay box for a further 8-9 hours.

Hay box recipes included:

- Oatmeal porridge: boil for 10 minutes, leave in box 8-10 hours
- Dried apple rings: boil for 10 minutes (after soaking for several hours), leave in box 5-6 hours or overnight

- Lentil soup: cook for 40 minutes, leave in box 5 hours
- Stews and hotpots: cook for 30 minutes, leave in box 4-5 hours
- Boiled beef: cook for 1 hour, leave in box 5-6 hours
- Potatoes: boiled in skins, leave in box 2-3 hours
- Boiled bacon: cook for 45 minutes; leave in box 4-5 hours.

Jam Jars

Jam jars were another economical way of cooking. Large stoneware jars were filled with prepared meat, vegetables and a steamed pudding, covered with greaseproof paper secured with string, and placed in a large-lidded pan of boiling water, regularly topped up to avoid 'boiling dry'.

Dorothy Hartley described the traditional system of cauldron cookery that may have been the precursor to the jam jar system. Extras such as carrots and turnips could be put in the water, or little bags containing haricot beans could be hung from the jars, and the whole lot cooked together in the water. This is very similar to the way that we steam our Christmas puddings today.

Casseroles

Casseroles were very popular in the early twentieth century. They came in new shades of buff, brown and green; in squat chunky shapes; were easy to keep clean; were fireproof; attractive enough to use 'oven to table'; and had no enamel to chip or wear off. They also saved on washing up – always a plus point. One of the best-known brands was Herbert's of Pentonville Road, London, who produced entrée, gratin, pie, divided, serving and roasting dishes, lidded stewpots, cafetières, decorated pitchers and much more besides.

Housewives keen to spruce up their dinner tables could buy matching sets at reasonable prices (a 3 pint casserole cost 2s in the late 1920s) or astute husbands could act on the hints in the Herbert's *Book of Casserole Cookery* and buy them as presents. Glass ovenware was also available. The best-known brands were Pyrex and Phoenix: a Phoenix glass entrée dish with a lid cost 7s 6d in the late 1930s.

Steamers

A set of steamers towering above the stove would have been a familiar sight in many kitchens. Food cooked by steam was said to be much healthier than food that was boiled, and as everything was cooked on one burner this method also saved money. Steamers were expensive – Florence Jack quoted 6s for a good one in 1914 – so housewives were encouraged to improvise with whatever was at hand. This might be a metal colander or a perforated trivet balanced over a pan, a greased plate with a second plate inverted over it, or a double boiler. Small chops or pieces of fish were steamed between greased plates over a pan of boiling water in which something else was cooking, and potatoes were suspended as in a hammock in muslin under the pan lid and above the water in which the meat was boiling. This method saved not only fuel but reduced the amount of washing up – a double boon to the housewife, who would get through four or more lots of washing-up in the course of a normal day. Fish, fruit, vegetables and meat could be steamed, and a meal made entirely in the steamer might comprise boiled chicken, parsley sauce, potatoes, cauliflower and canary pudding with apricot sauce. The canary pudding was cooked in a basin in the bottom tier of the steamer, and those parts of the meal that cooked quickly were put in the top tiers to avoid disturbing those that cooked slowly.

Some books referred to 'waterless cookers' as being similar to steamers. These waterless cookers seem to be what we now know as pressure cookers, and were treated with some respect because of their unpredictability.

MODERN HINT

A small collapsible steamer is easier to store and can be used as a colander – useful in a small kitchen.

Paper Bag Cookery

The paper bag system of cookery was popularised by Monsieur M. Soyer. It was said to be odourless, hygienic, labour-saving, economical, nutritious, prevented waste and simple to use. Cooking in paper was not new, but Soyer's system brought an economical way of cooking into the kitchen as a complete kit. Alternatively, if the housewife could not afford the kit she could do what housewives have done for years and improvise.

The paper manufacturer James Spicer produced the paper for the 'real' bags, marketed as 'Soyer bags' or Kookera bags.[67] Domestic greaseproof paper could – with a bit of folding, some advance greasing and small bulldog clips to seal the opening – be induced to serve the same purpose for a fraction of the price. The process was straightforward. A bag of the correct size was greased inside and the food inserted, the opening was sealed either by bulldog clips or a proprietary clip, and the bag was put into a preheated oven on a gridded shelf or rack (food put on a solid shelf would burn). To test whether the food was cooked, the housewife would prod it with a finger (or a skewer) or make a tiny hole in the bag to have a look.

The system is similar to modern boil-in-the-bag meals, and a great number of recipes were published during the inter-war period. As long as the bag was firmly sealed, it was possible to cook an Irish stew, small cakes and apple dumplings in paper bags; meals such as bacon and eggs were best avoided as frying was not possible. *Tried Favourites* hailed Mons. Soyer as 'a public benefactor', and included recipes for stewed apples, gooseberry pudding and roast chicken (stuffed and rubbed with butter, cooked in 40 minutes).[68]

Chafing Dish Cookery

The chafing dish was briefly in vogue during the 1910s and again during the 1930s. While seen primarily as a novelty item (one book refers to chafing-dish parties being popular in America in the 1910s), it was marketed as a valid and useful item for people in rooms with limited cooking facilities, a handy way to provide a hot snack after an evening out, a way to provide a hot meal while picnicking, shooting or yachting, and also for those catering for invalids. Its odd name is derived from the French word *chauffer*, to heat.

A basic chafing dish made from nickel could be bought for 12s in 1914, and consisted of an upper pan known as a blazer, a removable lower hot water pan, a stand and a methylated spirit lamp. Food could be cooked at the table (scrambled eggs, chicken livers on toast, canned foods), re-cooked (with a fresh sauce added) or kept warm until needed.

Chafing dish, 1914.

Used in conjunction with a hay box, dishes such as stewed fruit, pulses and milk puddings could be produced with considerable saving of fuel. The keen chafing-dish owner (who was also probably an amateur at everyday cooking) was advised to refrain from prolonged cooking preparation at table as it was very tedious for guests to have to sit through the fumbling and measuring that inevitably accompanied this unusually public style of cooking.

Many women living in 'rooms' (bedsits) had to cope with sketchy or non-existent cooking facilities. This is where the biscuit tin oven would have been handy. The woman who sent this tip to *Home Words* won a prize of 5*s*: 'I live in one room with only a gas ring for cooking, and find when boiling a pudding for one and a half hours, I can steam a mutton chop on an enamel plate on the top of the saucepan instead of a lid, and so save gas.'[69]

Perking-up Dull Meals

Mrs Peel, author of several cookery books for the struggling middle classes, had many suggestions for perking-up dull desserts, including colourful decorations such as glacé cherries, almonds, hundreds and thousands, and whipped cream. Plain prunes could be made more attractive by stewing them in water with a little carmine added and serving them, not as plain stewed prunes shovelled untidily into a bowl, but arranged in a ring with the pink syrup artfully poured over as a compote. She clearly had an eye for presentation, pointing out that the average boiled fish was not an attractive dish unless it was spruced up appropriately. Tapioca pudding, the bane of thousands of children, has always been one of the most difficult dishes to serve attractively. Mrs Peel suggested renaming it tapioca cream, and putting it in a glass bowl with a little cream, with half a cherry and four pieces of angelica as decoration. This would have been much more attractive, if not any more palatable.

Housewives catering for an elderly person were sometimes at a loss to know how to present individual meals, especially if they were different to those eaten by the rest of the family and there was not much money to 'stretch'. Serving small quantities in an attractive way might include preparing separate small syrup puddings or a portion of cabbage pressed into a teacup and turned out neatly on the plate.

Feeding children in hot weather could be difficult if the child was picky or the meals were unimaginative. A meal such as steak, boiled potatoes, vegetable marrow and jam roly-poly, for example, would be far better received in hot weather if a few changes were made. Sandwiches made with the meat cold and sliced very thinly, and lettuce and tomatoes, followed by stewed fruit and custard was one suggestion. Serving the meal outside picnic-style was another tip. Eating *al fresco* was an exciting experience, especially if the child had their own little chair and table or could sit with their mother outside.

However, even this innocuous-sounding menu could have its drawbacks unless it was carefully prepared. As one cookery book pointed out, some things are just not worth it: lukewarm rhubarb, in their opinion, was repellent whatever was done to it.[70]

Garnishing and Presentation

Simple garnishes were seen as perfectly acceptable as long as they were neatly cut (either with a knife or with a tin cutter) into uniform sizes and were not too eccentric. The majority of single-handed housewives would not have had time or money for fancy additions, but as Mrs Peel briskly pointed out, there was no need to dish things up carelessly.[71] Attractive presentation went a long way towards the enjoyment of a meal, and the housewife was urged to arrange things with care and attention. This needed a little forethought so that items were served on the correct sized dish and clashing or similar colours were avoided; it also meant ensuring that there was enough sauce, vegetables, etc., and generally taking a few pains to make the meal look attractive. Exhausted-looking mutton cutlets lounging around in a dish and a heap of spinach flopped into another dish did not look attractive.[72] Cabbage looked more appetising if it had been carefully drained beforehand and served piled up around a china strainer; and mashed potatoes looked much more attractive either riced, piled into fancy borders or scored with a fork before serving.

By the 1930s, ideas on garnishing and food decoration were beginning to lean towards the fanciful. Vegetables, raw or cooked, were cut into a variety of shapes; aspic jelly was used lavishly; fish scraps could be used to decorate fish dishes (oysters, prawns, scallops etc.); bread and pastry were cut into fancy shapes; breakfast rolls could be served tied with pink ribbon or arranged in a Prince of Wales fan; and silver skewers or hatelets were used, hatpin-style, to attach fancily-shaped pieces of vegetables to a variety of cold dishes.

In some cases, the more basic the dish, the more the need for decoration; hence clear Toledo soup (the ingredient was simply brown stock) was garnished with carrot stars and yellow and white custard crescents. Cutting cooked carrots into star shapes sounds fiddly enough, but the directions for the yellow custard crescent shapes seem almost surreal. Two egg yolks were beaten up with milk, coralline pepper (cayenne) and seasoning, and poached until firm; when cold, this mixture was cut into slices with a wet knife on wet paper, cut into crescent shapes with a vegetable cutter, washed several times in hot water and left in cold water until needed.

Housewives were constantly reminded to make mealtimes as attractive as possible for 'hubby'. On his return from work he might be treated to fish scallops garnished with lemon and parsley, liver cutlets, or meat fritters with gravy. A small illustration in *Home Cookery & Comforts* shows him, still in hat and overcoat, newspaper under one arm, removing dish covers, 'eager to see what there is for supper'.[73] Hopefully he also noticed the bowl of flowers, the shining glassware, the neatly ironed and starched tablecloth, and was eager to greet the wife who had probably washed, ironed and starched the cloth, arranged the flowers, set the table with shining glassware, and prepared and served the meal for him.

Some dishes were simply unattractive, whatever was done to them: boiled fish, tapioca and mince needed major renovation before being sent to table, but even Mrs Peel seemed unable to think of anything to do to improve untidy looking puddings such as jam

1 A well-equipped 1920s kitchen.

2 Interior of a middle-class grocery shop, 1904.

14 GLADSTONE ROAD, TUNBRIDGE WELLS

BEST VALUE TEA COMPANY, LIMITED

WILL OPEN THEIR NEW BRANCH AS ABOVE ON

THURSDAY, OCTOBER 30TH

TEA. COFFEE, AND COCOA

Direct from the Growers.

SAVE ALL INTERMEDIATE PROFITS!

☞ **SAMPLES FREE ON APPLICATION** ☜

GRANULATED SUGAR
YELLOW CRYSTAL SUGAR } $1\frac{1}{2}$**d.** per lb.
LOAF SUGAR

FOR A FEW DAYS ONLY

HANDSOME DECORATED FANCY TINS

Will be given away *without extra charge* with all TEAS at **1s. 6d.**
per lb. and upwards

BEST VALUE TEA COMPANY, LIMITED
14 GLADSTONE ROAD, TUNBRIDGE WELLS

3 Pricelist, 1904.

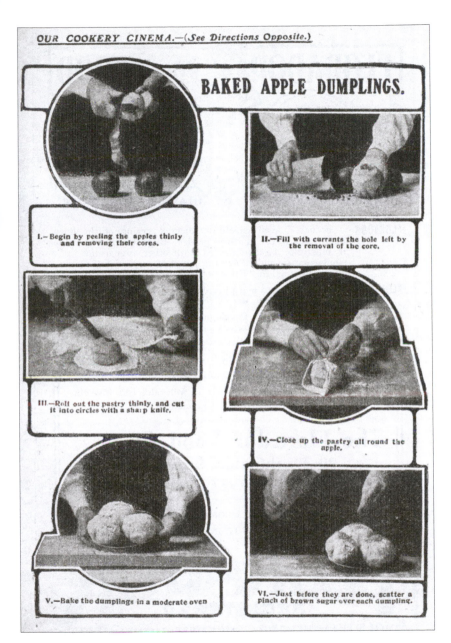

BAKED APPLE DUMPLINGS.

I.—Begin by peeling the apples thinly and removing their cores.

II.—Fill with currants the hole left by the removal of the core.

III.—Roll out the pastry thinly, and cut it into circles with a sharp knife.

IV.—Close up the pastry all round the apple.

V.—Bake the dumplings in a moderate oven

VI.—Just before they are done, scatter a pinch of brown sugar over each dumpling.

4 Cookery cinema, 1913.

FLORADOR DELICIOUS FOOD

The GREAT WHEAT FOOD
10 GOLD MEDALS

The PUREST FORM OF PERFECT NOURISHMENT

The Florador Food Co.   GLASGOW & LONDON

FLORADOR is prepared from carefully selected grains of the finest qualities of wheat in three grades—large, medium and fine. It must not be confounded with other preparations of a similar nature which lack the essential properties of nourishment contained in "FLORADOR."

FLORADOR is rich in nitrogen and phosphates; strengthens the system; is easily digested by sensitive stomachs.

FLORADOR may be served as Porridge, in Soups, Baked or Boiled Puddings, Blanc Mange, Cakes, etc., and is greatly relished by young and old alike.

Fine Grained Florador is specially adapted for Infants' Food

RECIPES ON EACH PACKET.

Of all Stores and Leading Grocers in ½-lb. and 1-lb. Packets. In 1s. Tins at Chemists'.

The Florador Food Co.,
90 Washington Street, Glasgow.

London Depot: COWAN & CO., College Street, E.C.

CHILDREN THRIVE ON FLORADOR FOOD. . . . REMEMBER TO ORDER IT IN YOUR NEXT PARCEL.

FLORADOR
REGISTERED

Awarded 10 Gold Medals and Prix d'Honneur, 1897 Cookery and Food Exhibition.

5 Advertisement for Florador pastry flour.

6 Herbert's casseroles.

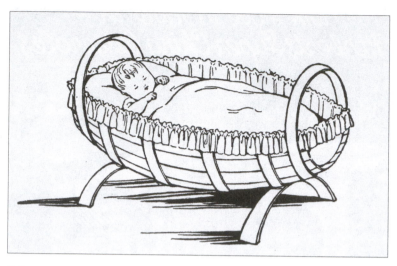

7 Barrel cradle, 1920s.

SAVOURY SUPPER DISHES.

Some tasty recipes for the winter supper table menu.

PEOPLE who have had a substantial midday meal don't need a heavy supper, nor would it be good for them, but they like something hot and tasty for the last meal of the day.

Give hubby some of these recipes, and see how pleased he'll be.

MEAT FRITTERS.

INGREDIENTS:

1 lb. of cold meat (minced)   Nutmeg (grated to taste)
1 lb. of breadcrumbs   Pepper to taste
6 oz. of butter   Salt to taste
2 finely chopped onions   3 eggs
A little flour.

Soak three-fourths of the breadcrumbs in cold water. Press the water out of the breadcrumbs. Fry the onions in butter for two or three minutes. Now add the breadcrumbs and the meat to the onions, and season with salt, pepper, and nutmeg.

Stir until the mixture is quite hot, add two-thirds of the beaten-up eggs, mix very quickly, and pour on to a dish to cool. Roll the mixture into the shape of small eggs. Dust them with flour, dip them in the remainder of the egg, then into breadcrumbs, and fry them in the remainder of the butter until a nice golden brown colour. Drain on kitchen paper. Serve with or without gravy.

Hubby will be eager to see what there is for supper after he has tasted one or two of these delicious recipes.

8 A husband at the dinner table, 1913.

9 Drying soap.

10 Vulcan gas oven with glass door.

11 Extravagant use of leftovers: petits paniers à la jardinière.

12 Ingenious use of ingredients: ouefs à l'anchois.

rolls. She suggested trimming the ends off, cutting the remainder into neat slices and sending the dish to the table dusted with sugar and arranged on a lace paper or doyley.

four

Thrift Around the House

The practice of thrift extended past frugal shopping and cooking, and was much more than a vague impulse to hold on to things that might come in useful sometime. A true practitioner of thrift saw virtue and new life in every discarded fishbone, pinecone and hot water bottle. In the 1920s and '30s, when many families were experiencing financial straits, housekeeping advice books and home sewing books contained a mass of detail on ingenious ways to use up discarded oddments. Everyday utility crafts such as knitting, quilting and rug making were often included, as well as renovations, resurrections, recycling, and rethinking, which are the subjects of this chapter.

Every woman was expected to know how to knit, sew, patch, darn and crochet, and most would also be confident tackling bigger projects such as dressmaking and making loose covers. Even the most inexperienced were encouraged to develop their creative skills: a booklet issued by the Singer company insisted that any woman could achieve wonders with scissors, tape measure and a sewing machine (a Singer, naturally) and amaze herself with her new-found skills. Author Julia Cairns even managed to bring in a hint that thrift could be fashionable, pointing out that attractive yet cheap curtains could be made from butter muslin, 6d per yard, dipped in cold tea.

Although many housewives found no time in a busy day for anything but the most essential darning and mending, it was sometimes possible for them to find a quiet moment for knitting or embroidery. Sometimes the children of the family might be roped in to help with sorting buttons, cutting rug scraps or holding wool while it was being wound. One activity might give the modern reader pause for thought:

> Some home economists [housewives] keep a cardboard box into which small shreds of woollen materials can be stored until sufficient are accumulated for stuffing a cushion. This is ... an excellent way of finding employment for very young children. In many infant schools the picking of shreds is one of the first methods of training in handwork.[74]

Quite apart from its associations with picking oakum, it is hard to imagine any child believing he or she will live long enough to actually pick enough shreds to stuff even the smallest cushion.

Even the most well-heeled households were urged to practice thrift. As one writer pointed out, 'the mistress of the house has it in her power to institute and regulate the thousand-and-one economies which are of such vital importance in keeping down household expenses'.[75] She advised turning sheets sides to middle, cutting worn parts from towels and making washcloths from the unworn parts, and making shabby and worn tablecloths into tray cloths and sideboard runners. She also recommended recycling old clothes, re-dyeing ribbons, using old gloves for dirty gardening-type jobs, re-trimming hats, re-curling feathers, and re-footing socks (and when the socks were completely beyond repair they were sewn together in threes and used as floor cloths). Glove tips made fingerstalls, old skirts made dusters and even old combinations could be made into handy cleaning cloths to use at spring cleaning time. Although we may not associate such economies with the middle classes today, these examples are by no means unique. Many affluent families struggled to retain their position among their peers and would in many cases have done practically anything to avoid losing caste at a time when a family's social position was dependent on such things as having the 'right' clothes and going to the 'right' parties.

Other hints included returning bottles and jars to claim the deposit back, saving bran (used as a packing material) and handy for all sorts of things from washing chintz to the popular bran tubs of children's parties, and tearing off the unused parts of letter paper for future use. Other economies were born simply from the need to provide bedding and clothes for the family, or household items either necessary or pretty – and sometimes both.

Bedding

Providing adequate bedding was not always easy, and there were many ways to improvise, alter or improve, such as:

- Bedspreads from faded or worn curtains
- Bolster slips, pillow cases, cot sheets, draw sheets, ironing sheets and dust sheets from old bed sheets
- Pram covers knitted from odd lengths of yarn
- Bed covers from old puttees (unpicked and sewn together onto a backing fabric), or from old silk stockings cut into ½in bias strips and knitted into squares

- Remnants of wool or cotton sewn into 8in squares sewn together back to back, stuffed with oddments, and sewn together in rows to make quilts

MODERN HINT

Make quilts or curtains from favourite outgrown dresses.

Clothes

Clothes were so voluminous that a variety of articles could be put together for children using old or outgrown adult clothes. It seems that nothing was discarded unless it had no further use – and then it probably appeared in a rag rug or quilt:

- Jerseys for children from old woollen stockings
- Children's bloomers from old stockings
- Old knitted scarves unpicked and the wool reused for darning
- A child's dress made from a curtain valance plus lace insertion (cost 1d per yard in the 1930s), or oddments of silk joined together with crochet

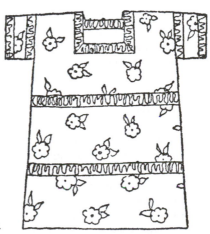

Child's dress, 1930s.

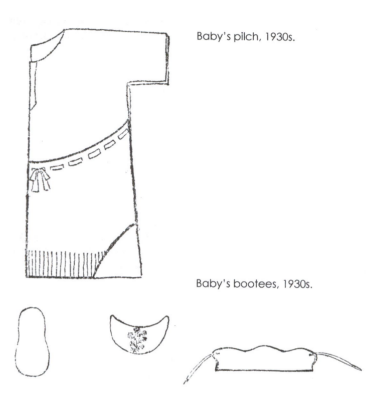

Baby's pilch, 1930s.

Baby's bootees, 1930s.

- Two baby's vests made from a pair of Celanese knickers (this probably says as much about the volume of contemporary knickers as it does about thrift)
- Baby's shoes from suede gloves, bootees from old silk socks

Household Items

Necessity was definitely the mother of invention when it came to ingenious uses for odd bits and pieces:

- A tea cosy from a trilby hat
- A kneeling mat from an old hot water bottle
- A bodkin from a shoelace tag
- Dishcloths from old string or pieces of lace curtain
- Mat from an old rope clothesline coiled and sewn

Hoarding

The thrifty housewife was urged to strike a balance between ruthless elimination of all dust-catching clutter and selective hoarding of potentially useful bits and pieces. Families accustomed to frequent moves between rented accommodation would not want to be burdened with surplus bits and pieces; this is one reason why family letters and photos do not always survive today (they were also used as spills and firelighters). Another reason was that cupboard space was often at a premium in new houses and items seen as old-fashioned or ugly were rarely harboured.

However, there were lots of things worth keeping. Writers urged women to chop up packing cases for kindling (chopping wood, according to an old saying, warms you twice), and to pass on old clothes to charities. Old rags and paper were disposed of either by burning or selling them to rag-and-bone men – although opinion was divided on the benefits of having old rags lying around the house. Finally, empty jam jars were useful around the house, so some large jars were kept back for use in the kitchen and others were returned for the deposit (6d-1s to was refunded on large jars in 1910).

Economies of all kinds were enforced during the First World War (no throwing rice at weddings, no feeding wild birds and stray animals), and many writers continued to offer thrifty advice through the 1920s and 1930s when money and resources were tight and materials scarce.

For those inclined more to hoarding than to eliminating there was plenty of scope for creative action in housekeeping advice books. Modern purists may wince at 1930s suggestions for making bookcases and medicine chests from antique clocks and cutting the legs off old-fashioned sideboards, but other suggestions were extremely practical. The four-volume *Book of the Home*, published in 1928, included directions for making a cradle from a beer barrel and a cot from a banana crate. Banana crate cots had also been mentioned in the classic account of working-class London life, *Round About a Pound a Week* (1913) – a strange irony that rich and poor alike were being urged to make use of the same humble wooden box!

Among the many solutions for the creative use of oddments are these:

- Beech leaves: beds for the poor – said to be 'very springy'[76]
- Bran: stuffing for pin cushions; packing eggs (short term) or china, cleaning embroidery and copper

- Broom head (worn out): cut in half to make 2 hearth brushes
- Candle ends: melt and mix with turpentine to make floor polish; melt and introduce lengths of string to make tapers
- Chaff: stuffing mattresses
- Chocolate box: jewellery box
- Corks: cut into fancy shapes to decorate picture frames
- Cork pieces: stuff a homemade lifebelt
- Corset steel: shoe tree
- Cotton reels: doorstop; children's toy; threaded on wire to make an ornament for an overmantel
- Cradle: log basket
- Dandelions: wine; salad; medicine; roots, flowers and leaves boiled up to make furniture polish
- Diamanté: stick broken pieces on driving gloves to make sparkly reflectors
- Fish bones: save, clean and arrange in artistic groups as a novel ornament
- Grandfather clock: a medicine chest made by removing the works and fitting shelves inside
- Hot water bottles: cut up to make mats for flowerpot bases; tack strips to brooms to reduce wear on skirting boards and doors; kneeling mat; insoles for walking shoes
- Letters: firelighters; warm lining or backing for patchwork quilts
- Newspaper: singeing poultry to remove feathers; firelighters
- Packing cases: make into cabinets, escritoires or ottomans; chop up for firewood
- Paper bags: jam jar covers
- Pine cones: kindling
- Postcards: spills
- Rolling pin: cover with wadding and use as storage for face veils
- Soap: save scraps and melt for use when washing up
- String: oddments knitted together to make dish cloths
- Old trilby: a tea cosy
- Tea leaves: clean glass, mirrors, bottles and carpets (scattered when damp so they stuck to the dust and got swept up when the room was cleaned)
- Toothbrush: spring cleaning; applying black lead
- Tyres: cut strips to use as rubber bands
- Wooden meat skewers: poke out dirt from picture frames

Shoes

Household items, particularly clothes and shoes, were repaired over and over again. Many fathers became adept at mending boots and shoes, and some owned lasts and other shoemaking tools to make the job easier and more professional. The hints offered in the thriftiest books are clearly aimed at households where every farthing had to be counted. For example:

- Children's boots: split toecaps repaired with pieces of old kid glove stuck to the inside of the boot with liquid cement, polished when dry
- Waterproofing for boots: 2 parts beeswax mixed with 1 part mutton fat
- Brown shoes: rub with a banana skin or lemon juice and milk
- Repair tagless bootlaces: sew linen thread or thick silk, twist tightly round the tagless end
- Substitute shoe trees: rolled paper

Possessions also had to be kept in good condition: people may be poor, as someone remarked, but they don't necessarily have to look poor. A great deal of energy and ingenuity was spent on ensuring that the family looked as respectable as possible. As one book put it, when offering hints for keeping husbands tidy, 'To act as your husband's valet is neither beneath your dignity nor is it spoiling him. It is true economy.'[77] These hints would have been particularly applicable during the Depression when many husbands were desperately seeking work and needed to look well groomed:

- Copal varnish applied to the soles of new shoes was said to make them last longer (copal was a resin used as a varnish)
- Lemon juice was used as a substitute for shoe polish
- White buckskin boots: cleaned with a mix of 1lb bathbrick, 2lb pipeclay, 4oz pumice stone powder and 6oz ox gall, all made into balls and rubbed over the boots
- Dubbin: 1 pint boiled linseed oil, 1oz Burgundy pitch, 3oz each spirits of turpentine and beeswax
- Renovate navy or black serge: rub with a mixture of ivy leaves steeped in boiling water
- New comb: wash it in soapy water and rub sweet oil into it before using

- Reproof raincoats: a mixture of alum and sugar of lead
- Frayed trouser cuffs: make an edging from joined-together strips cut from old kid gloves, fold it double and attach to the inside of the hem
- To clean light-coloured cloth gaiters (as worn by children): rub with grated potato, the more liquid the better
- Woollen skirts: wear back to front on alternate days to ensure even wear
- Homemade linen buttons (used as substitutes for decorative buttons on washing day as they were less likely to break when garments were mangled): a 2in square of calico, its four points folded in and stitched, folded in half and half again to form a ¼in square button which was then buttonhole-stitched around the edge. Alternatively, linen buttons were available at haberdashery shops but most households would have had a few oddments of calico put aside in the scrap bag

Yet another strand of thrift encompasses the saving of money and resources by adopting various practical measures around the house. Such measures were generally only an option for the more affluent, but as many books pointed out, it was amazing how much money was saved by paying attention to small details.

MODERN HINT

Save 20p coins. They're small enough not to be missed, easy to spot and can be accumulated very quickly.

Some experts felt that the installation of a water softening plant would save large amounts of money otherwise spent on softening agents such as soda, much used in laundry work in pre-detergent days. Others felt that having live-in maids wasted space, took away privacy, cost too much, and advocated either daily maids, who lived off the premises, or no maids at all. Hiring a professional firm to spring clean the house was said to save both money and time, as was paying a firm to overhaul the household's electrical appliances once a year. Ideas on house decoration were also changing as the first faint noises of the labour-saving drive began to make themselves heard: women who had done little housework found themselves suddenly confronted with acres of polished floors, rooms full of knick-knacks and furniture requiring daily cleaning and polishing. Decorative features such as oak panelling were ruled to be pointless extravagance and a waste of time, as few people would have such a thing anywhere in the house if they had to polish it themselves.

One writer with particularly firm opinions on the subject of thrift was Matilda Lees-Dods, author of *The Ideal Home*. She felt that newly married couples should think long and hard about every single purchase, and pointed out that no household, however well-heeled, should waste anything that came into it. She was particularly concerned with matters that still affect modern homes, such as saving electricity. She recommended that houses newly wired for electricity should have the switches placed as close to doors as possible as this made it easy to turn the lights off when leaving the room. A further measure to encourage economy was to install a master switch so that the lights in the maids' rooms were turned off at a fixed hour – no more reading in bed and wasting current.

Other measures were more modest but would have made a big difference to the housekeeping budget:

- New bottom for an aluminium saucepan: a sponge cake tin of the same diameter fitted inside the pan
- Mending an enamel saucepan: add either a tin patch or put a drop of solder inside and out (this would probably have been lead solder which is not safe for food use)
- Cleaning balls: 1oz powdered chalk, 5oz powdered pipe clay, 2oz spirits of wine, made into small balls and used for spot cleaning of clothes
- Mending tears in clothes: a needle threaded with a hair was said to produce an invisible repair
- Mend a cracked washbasin: paint along the crack, tape over the paint and paint over this
- Broken coal scuttle: put a piece of lino in the bottom
- Broken china: fix edges together with white lead (again, not safe for food use)
- Homemade flypaper: 1½oz castor oil heated gently with 2oz resin, spread either on sheets of paper or on wires with paper cups attached to catch drips
- Broken glass dishes: fix edges together with water-glass (the same substance used for preserving eggs)
- Substitute hot water bottle: a brick, heated and placed in a flannel bag, or a bag of fine dry sand heated in the oven
- Substitute for an iron: a hot water bottle

The Gloucester Road
School *of* Cookery

109A, GLOUCESTER ROAD,
SOUTH KENSINGTON,
LONDON, S.W.
(Established 1894.)

Classes held daily in Household, Invalid,
High-class Cookery and Confectionery.

Students trained in all branches of
Cookery, also in practical teaching and
demonstrating. Courses from six weeks
to six months. Certificates granted.

Short Courses of six, twelve, and twenty-
four lessons in Household or High-Class
Cooking.

Special Courses for Cake-making and
Confectionery.

All the newest dishes taught.

Demonstration Lectures three times
weekly—1/- and 1/6 each.

Prospectus on application to the Principal.

Advertisement for Gloucester Road School of Cookery, 1913.

- A new mop head: cut off the old fabric and replace with hanks of knitting cotton, then cover with strong material
- Preserve a bath sponge: cover it with a bag knitted from fine cotton. Said to prolong the life of the sponge by an impressive six years
- Clean a wire mattress: puff at it with a bicycle pump
- Clean glazed chintz curtains: rub dry bran in well with a piece of flannel

- Furniture polish: roots, flowers and leaves of dandelions boiled up in a pan of water
- To clean furniture: 1 teacup of paraffin in a pail of hot water
- Imitation ground glass: as much Epsom salts as can be dissolved in a little hot water, and painted over the window while still hot
- Homemade fire extinguisher: 3lb of salt put into 1 gallon of water with 1½lb sal ammoniac added, stored in a bottle
- Soap: cut up blocks of soap and leave them to dry out

In many households thrift was seen and taken for granted as an essential part of domestic solvency. Housewives might not have worked outside the home, but they were certainly expected to work hard inside it. Whether trained by their mothers, in school or college, or at housecraft classes as married women, the average housewife was responsible for a wide variety of tasks and expected to be proficient in a range of skills, from decorating to baking; buying wholesome food; knitting socks, jumpers and scarves; making coal briquettes from coal dust moistened with paraffin; doing the family wash; mending, darning and patching; and generally doing their best to keep the family fed, healthy and respectable. This had to be done year in, year out with the knowledge that missing a day's washing and cleaning would mean extra hard work to catch up later. Housekeeping was one of the most relentless jobs a woman could do, simply because it never ended – there was always something else to do.

Advice books included timetables because it made sense to have the day mapped out: washing on Monday and ironing on Tuesday meant that clothes were clean for Sunday, and baking at the end of the week meant a little leisure and a few nice treats for tea at the weekend. Many husbands helped with the heavy jobs such as getting the coal in, distempering and decorating etc., and children were often raised to far greater levels of independence than is the case today. However, for many housewives life was one long struggle against dirt, poverty and insecurity, and Walter Greenwood spoke for all housewives when he quoted the young housewife who said that, 'Trying to be respectable on a limited income means that you've always to be watching pennies'.[78]

five

The First World War

In one of the cookery books published in the early 1920s is a remark that thrift in catering was one of the most useful things learned by housewives during the First World War. A booklet published during the war was rather more direct, stating that, 'every ounce of food wasted helps to make food dearer, and so to make the nation poorer, and less able to bear the enormous burden which the war is throwing on all alike'.[79]

This chapter discusses some of the domestic problems that faced Britain's housewives during the First World War. Every household, no matter what class or income, was expected to behave in a patriotic and responsible way and to avoid extravagance, waste and ostentation. Many thousands of families had no choice but to watch every penny, but for those enjoying a high level of income a definition of extravagance might have included pretty underwear, cut flowers, out-of-season fruit or expensive wines. In addition, many people felt that the huge amount of raw materials used in the manufacture of wines, beers and spirits could have been put to far better use. Despite the vigorous work of the country's temperance societies, alcohol abuse was still widespread at the turn of the century, and the National Food Economy League estimated that the nation's 'drink bill' was £160-£170 million per year. In 1906 the figure had been estimated at £166,425,911, or £33 16s 3d per head.[80]

Budgeting

Government figures published at the end of the war showed an increase of 90% (maximum) in weekly expenditure on food for working-class families, with unskilled families faring worse than those with a skill or trade. According to these figures, the percentage increase in expenditure averaged out as:

- 67% for skilled class (weekly expenditure 1914: 49s 3d, weekly expenditure 1918: 82s 4d)
- 81% for unskilled class (weekly expenditure 1914: 36s 4d, weekly expenditure 1918: 65s 10d)[81]

Other sources pointed to the very poor, to people on small fixed incomes, and to the professional classes as faring the worst during the war. Sylvia Pankhurst said bluntly that people were starving in the East End of London because they couldn't afford to buy food at inflated prices.[82] The authors of *the Eat-Less-Meat Book* (1917) pointed out that a healthier diet (less meat, sugar and flour, more cheap and healthy foodstuffs) was a positive benefit to those areas of society accustomed to rich food, and showed that the 'voluntary rationing' scheme recommended by Lord Devonport could be achieved with very little disturbance to normal domestic rhythm and much benefit to digestive rhythm.

Shopping

Housewives were advised to shop in person and to pay cash; to select goods with an eye to nutrition, economy, season and price; and plan meals in advance where possible. Knowledge was definitely power when it came to food shopping and cooking.

MODERN HINT

This is still true. Being aware of basic nutrition, seasonal food and economical recipes as well as current issues such as air miles and future water shortages are all part of the consumer's concerns.

Leftovers could be used in the next day's meals, and meat (chosen considering availability and the method of cooking to be used, i.e. stewing) could be eked out with cheap, filling carbohydrates such as macaroni or suet pudding. Other staples recommended by cookery books included barley meal, which was used to make porridge, scones and bread, and oatmeal (used to make porridge, oatcakes, savoury dishes of all types, and thickening for soups and stews).

There were various ways to ensure that housewives took notice of specific products, one of the most effective being advertising. Some products, such as Nestle Milk, Daren Bread and Calder's Yeast were angled directly at women worried about nutrition, while other firms boasted of their superiority and were disparaging of rival products. The wholesale firm R. Lehmann & Co. recommended its skimmed, sweetened, condensed milk for use in porridge, milk puddings, bread and butter, and stated that: 'In tea it has not the mawkish flavour of Full-Cream milks' (in this context, 'mawkish' meant having a sickly-sweet flavour). An advert for Clark's Optimus Coffee Extract succeeded in covering every base possible. It saved time, money and waste; it helped disabled soldiers; and its use combined 'Patriotism, Thrift and Epicureanism' all at once.[83]

Careful shopping could sometimes yield pleasant surprises – pineapples for 1s 6d just after Christmas compared with 3-4s just before. However, in general, most food shopping was seen as much less of a pleasure: queues blighted life, choice was limited, ingredients disappeared and reappeared, and many women had to resort to planting a child in a queue in one shop while they themselves went to queue in another.

Cooking

The National Food Economy League pointed out that the traditional methods of cooking – frying, baking and boiling – were all wasteful or uneconomical. The league's list of thrifty alternatives included stewing, steaming, poaching (for fish), and using earthenware jars, two plates or a hay box. Thrifty cooking comprised such measures as:

- Keeping the water in which green vegetables, rice, pulses and macaroni had been cooked, and using it in soup or stock
- Making soup as often as possible to use up leftovers
- Stewing slowly rather than frying meat (although if frying was done the fat could be strained and reused several times)
- Keeping meat bones for stock
- Using a hay box to cook stews, soups and porridge (it could also be used for cleaning burnt pans, keeping the teapot hot and removing fruit stains from clothes). When not in use it could be covered with a pretty fabric and used in the living room as an extra seat
- Cooking between two plates or in jam jars (e.g. stewing fruit, making beef tea or broth)
- Seeking out economical and nutritious recipes, and planning meals carefully

- Baking with wholemeal rather than white flour or using barley flour
- Combining meat 50:50 with other ingredients such as potatoes, macaroni or oatmeal
- Keeping the outer leaves of vegetables, etc., for soup
- Boiling potatoes in their skins – peeling was said to waste 4oz per lb if done with a heavy hand (knives were commonly used for peeling at this time)
- Using home produce where available (chickens, eggs, fruit, herbs)
- Using cheap cuts of meat such as ox cheek, liver, tripe, or breast of mutton. Rabbits, said to be plentiful all over the country, were a good substitute for chicken
- Saving the trimmings from fish and using them to make the accompanying sauce (this also saved milk)
- Poaching fish
- Making all jam, etc., at home
- Replacing butter where possible with margarine or nut butters such as Nutter.

MODERN HINT

Using cheap cuts of meat, making jam and growing tomatoes, herbs and strawberries is satisfying and thrifty at the same time. Learning a few self-sufficiency skills means that we rely less on society for our survival and more on ourselves.

Leftovers

Even the most well-managed households tended to accumulate some leftovers of meat, fish, vegetables, fruit juice, cheese and fat. Wartime cookery books, drawing on older thrifty sources, provided lots of ideas for using them up, such as:

- Meat: served up again the next day cut into neat slices with salad, or made into curry, hash or a pie
- Bones: used for stock until exhausted (at this point bones developed holes and were of no further culinary use)
- Sauce or gravy: drops added to another dish

- Bacon scraps: added to vegetables, soups and stews
- Bacon rind: useful for flavouring soup
- Fish: made into fishcakes or pies
- Fish cooking water: fish soups or accompanying sauce
- Vegetables: add to salad, reheat and serve again or curry
- Potatoes (mashed): add to cheese, meat or fish dishes, or pastry
- Juice from fruit tarts: add to custard and gelatine and pour into a wetted mould until set
- Cheese rinds and oddments: washed, scraped and melted down for grating
- Fat: clarified and stored for frying and browning meat.

A particularly thrifty housewife might have acted on a hint offered in the *Victory Cookery Book*, where a use was found for the small amount of vinegar left in an emptied pickle bottle. A new pickle was made using the leftover vinegar, plus enough to cover carrot, cauliflower, etc., plus a few small onions and, after four boilings and a lot of standing, the new pickle was ready. It is debatable how much goodness remained in the vegetables after this treatment, or how much fuel was wasted when it might have been simpler to just pour the leftover liquid down the sink and eat the vegetables at the next meal.[84]

Bread was particularly prone to careless use in families where it was not a staple food. An 'Eat Less Bread' campaign started in May 1917 was endorsed by King George V. People were invited to sign a pledge agreeing to reduce consumption by a quarter and avoid using wheat flour in pastry (which is why so many other grains such as maize, barley and oats were recommended instead). Many families at this time were struggling with increased food prices due to shortages, and had so little to eat that bread was their staple food anyway, so reducing consumption was only an option for those on higher wages. The campaign's propaganda, linked to the contemporary ideas on 'voluntary rationing', included some interesting statistics regarding everyday waste of crumbs: 1 teaspoonful saved per family = 40,000 tons of bread per year – and slices: one slice wasted once a day by 48,000,000 British people.[85]

Advice offered by cookery books included making bread at home where possible (adverts for flour and yeast appeared in the NFEL handbook), not eating new bread (bad for the digestion and difficult to cut), and using up all crusts.

Meat Dishes

Many households simply could not afford to eat meat before, during or after the First World War, and housewives who could afford to buy meat found that they had to learn to use the cheaper cuts, which were often those that were traditionally eaten by the working classes. Thrifty housewives had long been urged to use cuts such as pig's feet and cow's heels, and wartime menus in cookery books included dishes such as sheep's head broth (plus barley and mixed vegetables), liver pudding, and stewed pigs' feet (with turnip, onion and carrot).

Another way of serving meat was to eke out a small piece with a cheaper but more filling ingredient, such as oatmeal or vegetables. Recipes included meat roll made with mince (extended with breadcrumbs), shepherd's pie, beans and bacon (made with scraps plus haricot beans) or salt pork and pease pudding (1lb of leg of pork, onion, carrot and half a large turnip).

Writing for the well-to-do who were accustomed to eating meat up to three times a day, Mrs C.S. Peel included what she called 'semi-meatless' menus in her *Eat-Less-Meat Book* (1917). This was published during the 'voluntary rationing' period when meat was in good supply for those who could afford it. She suggested buying a 7lb piece of silverside and removing a small piece for beef olives (Saturday dinner), and another piece for steak pie (Tuesday dinner). Sunday dinner was braised beef (about 5lb), with what was leftover served cold on Monday with the oddments made into croquettes on Wednesday. The second meat was rabbit: jugged on Thursday (with onion and forcemeat balls), pie on Friday (with macaroni and two eggs if cheap), and the third was 2lb of scrag end of neck of mutton for Scotch barley broth on the following Saturday. This system meant that the children had meat every other day at lunch, the adults had meat every other day at dinner, and there was very little waste or leftovers.

Fish

The price of fish went up and down week by week during the war, and the cheapest (according to one book) were haddock, herring, skate (sometimes available from market barrows) and ling (6d-8d per lb at one point). Herring was said to be the most nourishing as well as the cheapest. Dried fish was available, and R. Lehmann & Co. advertised canned herrings in tomato sauce, brisling in oil or tomato sauce, and salmon at 8½d per 1lb tin. However, the book that included the Lehmann advert stated that people should eat less canned salmon because it often contained 'a peculiarly dangerous poison if the canning should be imperfect'– the modern reader can only wonder who won this particular battle.[86] Fish recipes included:

- Baked stuffed haddock: 2lb haddock plus 2oz breadcrumbs, 1oz chopped suet, 1 dessertspoon chopped parsley, 1 egg, and seasoning
- Kedgeree: 8oz cooked fish, 4oz rice, a hard-boiled egg (if available), 2oz butter, and seasoning
- Fish pie: 8oz cold fish shredded with 4 large mashed potatoes or 4oz cooked rice, ¼ pint milk, 1oz butter or dripping, and 1 egg.

The *Victory Cookery Book* (1918) provided thirty pages of recipes and information that were probably relevant only for the purses of the more prosperous of households. Cod heads appeared in two recipes:

- Fish mock turtle soup: 1 cod's head, onions, carrot, oil, 1 lemon, basil, marjoram, 1 garlic clove, bay leaf, thyme, peppercorns, allspice, coriander, parsley stalks, water and baked flour (few other than middle-class households would have kept such a variety of spices and herbs in the kitchen cupboard)
- Fish cream soup: 1 cod's head, rice flour, milk, nutmeg and paprika or cayenne, plus rice to garnish.

There was fish pie, fish sausages, pan fish (fish gratin), halibut portugaise, eels Russian style, and much else. The correct method of opening and using a can of salmon was described (open it at the side and tip it out, reserving the best pieces for gratin dishes, the next best for salads and scallops, the smaller pieces for fishcakes and the oddments for sandwiches). Can openers would have been of the naked hooked blade variety that were often attached to a handle adorned with a bull's head – cans were less opened than ripped apart, leaving jagged edges and, not infrequently, bleeding fingers.

Sugar and Sweet Dishes

British people ate enormous quantities of sugar before the war, and many babies were reared on a mixture of cow's milk, sugar and water. Housewives were advised that soft brown sugar was just as good, and cheaper, than white. As an alternative (and when available) either dried fruit such as figs and dates, or syrup and honey, could be used – although 'dates, with no sugar, are good but ugly'.[87] Condensed milk was another useful sweetener. Granulated sugar was said to be just as good as loaf sugar for jam making (the addition of rhubarb juice would make homemade jams go further without detracting from the taste), and castor sugar was too expensive to be used regularly.

Jam itself could be used to make jam: a recipe for Beetroot Jam comprised beetroot, sago, almond essence, cochineal and raspberry jam. Beetroot in turn was an ingredient in imitation redcurrant jelly (tapioca, grated beetroot, forced rhubarb, and sugar).[88]

Save It

Economical cooking methods were essential during the war as fuel supplies diminished. Cookery books recommended the use of casseroles, earthenware and steamers of various types, and the hay box was seen as one of the most useful items in the kitchen. One handy tip from Belgium involved filling a dish or tin with water and then emptying it out just before the food was put in: this was said to be more effective than the traditional practice of greasing and it saved a tiny bit of margarine or butter. The wealthy were advised to eat less, the poor to learn economical methods of shopping and cooking, and everyone was urged to eke out what they had and learn to do the best with it. Economy was especially necessary around the house as shortages began to affect more and more people. Housewives would perhaps have turned to their thrifty household advice books and cookery books for useful hints and tips from previous generations.

Coal Economies:

These were legion, because the majority of houses had coal fires, and many had coal ranges. Wartime cookery books suggested that:

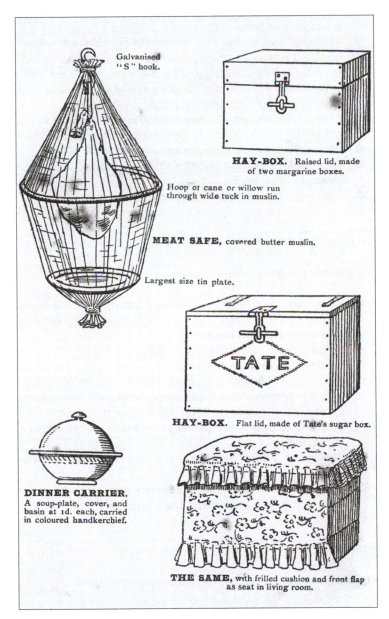

Galvanised
"S" hook.

HAY-BOX. Raised lid, made
of two margarine boxes.

Hoop of cane or willow run
through wide tuck in muslin.

MEAT SAFE, covered butter muslin.

Largest size tin plate.

TATE

HAY-BOX. Flat lid, made of Tate's sugar box.

DINNER CARRIER.
A soup-plate, cover, and
basin at 1d. each, carried
in coloured handkerchief.

THE SAME, with frilled cushion and front flap
as seat in living room.

Meat safe, hay box and dinner carrier, First World War.

- The range plus its pots, pans and utensils should be kept free from soot at all times
- All cinders were riddled and reused, the ash being dampened and used in place of emery paper to burnish steel fenders, etc.
- Throwing several buckets of water over coal in the coal cellar or spraying the coal with a strong solution of washing soda was rumoured to make the coal last longer
- Coal dust moistened with paraffin and bulked out with a small amount of clay made handy 'briquettes' to bank up a fire
- Filling some of the available space with fire bricks
- A large piece of chalk put at the back of the fire was said to give out a great heat
- Coal broke cleanly if each lump was broken individually

Gas Economies

The following were suggested to save gas:

- Fitting a square of sheet iron over the smallest burner effectively doubled the available cooking space. It was also useful for heating flat irons for laundry work
- Keeping all the parts of the oven clean
- Using thin utensils where possible
- Using a biscuit tin as an oven if only one dish was being cooked – this handy device, which appeared many times over in thrifty cookery books, could be fitted with a sheet of asbestos in the base and placed over a burner to cook a piece of meat or a small pudding
- Turning the gas off as soon as the pan was lifted from the burner
- Using candles at night was more thrifty than lighting the gas hours before it was needed and turning it down

Firewood

These tips aimed to reduce the amount of firewood used:

- Firewood dried overnight on top of the range took light more quickly (therefore saving wood) than wood that was lit while damp

- Half-burnt matches (struck once), dried potato peelings, or dried orange skins could all be used instead of wood to start a fire
- Country dwellers could forage for twigs and save money on bundles of chopped wood
- Packing cases cost 3d and would yield far more wood than the equivalent amount of sticks

Paper

Housewives were also encouraged to save paper:

- 5 sheets of newsprint (each one rolled from corner to corner, rolled up and the ends tucked in) were enough to light a sitting-room fire
- Newsprint was good for polishing windows, cleaning stove tops, brasses and steel items, and for giving the final polish to boots and shoes
- Using a cheaper notepaper saved money

Cleaning materials:

The price of all soaps increased during the war so economies had to be made. These included:

- using finely powdered sand for scrubbing tables, chairs, pastry boards etc. (thoroughly rinsed)
- collecting oddments of soap in a jar, covering with water and melting: the soap jelly was good for washing silver and was cheaper than soap powder
- buying in bulk where possible and spreading the bars out to dry: soap treated this way goes hard and lasts far longer than soap kept in the wrapper
- homemade cleaning preparations were said to be half the price of shop equivalents: a brass cleaner could be made from whiting, ammonia, water and oxalic acid

Cleaning economies

- a linoleum polish could be made from beeswax and turpentine
- a cheap furniture cream: turpentine, castile soap, white wax and beeswax
- a liquid furniture cream: butter of antimony, meths, linseed oil and white vinegar

MODERN HINT

The (to our grandmothers) mythical properties of elbow grease, along with lemon juice and bicarbonate of soda are traditionally said to clean almost everything in the modern home. Proprietary cleaners last much longer if used sparingly.

Laundry Economies

The following tips were suggested to save on laundry expenses:

- Doing the washing fortnightly instead of weekly might save soap, starch and firing (but would have produced far more washing)
- Upper-class men were asked to cut down on the number of dress shirts they used – soft shirts were much easier to wash and iron
- Upper-class women were asked to forgo labour-intensive flounces and fancy trimmings on underwear
- Children's clothes were ideally made with fewer ruffles and trimmings

Shortages

At various times meat, butter, cheese, sugar, potatoes and wheat flour were all 'short'. Housewives were exhorted to buy bacon for the week in one piece and boil it, use the water for stock, save the rising fat, and cut and fry rashers as needed. They were also encouraged to make rissoles with oatmeal instead of meat; to use nut butters or margarine instead of butter; to make cottage cheese (a very complicated and long-winded procedure described by Mrs

Peel; to make jam with salt and thicken with sago; to use ground rice and flaked maize when potatoes were scarce; and to use mashed potatoes (when available) or any grain flour when wheat flour was unobtainable.[89]

Substitutes

Ingenious ways to cook with what were known as 'substitutes' meant that some recipes were perhaps less palatable and well-received than others. They included:

- Bananas: savoury banana rissoles could be made from green bananas boiled, minced and mixed with flour until dry enough to shape into rissoles, then dipped in egg-and-breadcrumbs and fried in nut butter
- Banana flour: used to make buns, scones and Swiss rolls
- Potato flour: used for small cakes and scones
- Other flour alternatives: barley flour, maize flour or oatmeal could be substituted to make bread when wheat flour was short
- Oatmeal: used to replace meat
- Gravy substitutes: browning a tablespoon of sugar in an iron pan and then boiling it up in half a pint of water
- Jam substitutes: saccharin, honey, salt or substances called Consyp or Sypgar could be used [90]
- Cocoa butter and cotton-seed oil: used in cakes
- Cocoa butter: melted, heated, cooled and added to olive oil, honey and annatto (a yellow food colouring), shaped into pats and sent to table. It could also be made into a spread for children
- Nut butter: to replace butter; added to soups, puddings, cakes, scones, biscuits, salad dressing and much else
- Cream of tartar substitutes: supplies from France being unobtainable, various substitutes made from tartaric acid and rice flour, vinegar and baking soda, or simply using buttermilk, were recommended. Some grocers sold cream powder, which was said to be a good substitute
- Baking powder substitutes: made from tartaric acid, carbonate of soda plus cornflour or ground rice

Timeline of Rations and Shortages in the First World War

1914

- **4 August:** war declared, food hoarding begins
- **7 August:** maximum prices fixed for, among other staples, granulated sugar (4½*d* per lb), butter (1*s* 6*d* per lb), margarine (8*d* per lb)
- **10 August:** Anti-Hoarding Act passed but not enforced
- Women's Freedom League set up a cost-price restaurant in Nine Elms, London, and sold 250 meals per day
- **Late 1914/early 1915:** rent demonstrations in Glasgow

1915

- **January:** demands for government control of basic foodstuffs and prices
- **February:** increased food prices for flour (up 75%), home-produced meat (up 6%), imported meat (up 12%), sugar (up 72%), and coal (up 15%)
- **April-December:** government begins to commandeer ships
- **28 April-1 May:** Congress of Women's International League for Permanent Peace at the Hague
- **June:** food prices rising (butter up 2½*d*, cheese up 3*d*)
- **October:** thousands of women on rent strike in Glasgow leads to first ever British Rent Restrictions Act

1916

- **June:** food situation beginning to cause problems, exacerbated by U-boat campaign
- **August:** Food Department established
- **October:** Walter Runciman (President of the Board of Trade) denied that there was a need for rationing
- **November:** war bread introduced (extraction rate 76%)
- **21 November:** a Milk Order comes into force
- **7 December:** Lloyd George replaces Asquith as Prime

Minister, and the new government creates five new departments including Food and Food Production. Basics such as coal, sugar, potatoes and margarine in short supply, and the new Food Controller, Lord Devonport (of wholesale grocery firm Kearley & Tonge), exhorts the nation to eat less meat and get used to wholemeal bread (government bread). It was estimated that people were eating £50,000 worth of meat every day

- **9 December:** publication of 'The Food Supply of the United Kingdom' as confidential document
- sugar prices up 163%, eggs up 82%
- Labour government imposes restrictions on portion sizes in hotels and restaurants
- Savings and Savoury Dishes published in book form (originally published as a series of pamphlets), and The Patriotic Food League disbands with the introduction of the Ministry of Food
- Poor potato harvest causes further shortages

1917

- **February:** Lord Devonport's appeal for voluntary rationing falls largely on deaf ears (4lb bread, 2½lb meat, 12oz sugar per head per week). People told not to eat rhubarb leaves as they were poisonous when cooked. War bread extraction rate up to 81%
- **March:** Food Hoarding Order implemented
- **Spring:** U-boat campaign seen as major threat – only 3-4 weeks' food left in country
- **Spring:** a bottling and canning drive was arranged by the Board of Agriculture
- **April:** government takes over flour mills, Lord Devonport's 'Meatless Day' campaign starts
- **8 April:** coal, bread and potato queues in south London, paper shortage
- **May:** launch of 'Eat Less Bread' campaign
- **May:** Lord Devonport resigns, replaced by Lord Rhondda (ex-Army Contracts Dept)
- **21 May:** first National Kitchen at Westminster Bridge Road, London, opened by Queen and Princess Mary – 535 open within a year

- **September:** bread prices fixed and price control introduced for meat, heralding the beginning of rationing – many butchers said to close shops in protest
- **September:** farmer fined £5,500 plus £250 costs for selling potatoes above maximum price
- **Autumn:** convoy system introduced, losses cut by approximately one third
- **October:** bakers permitted to add 1lb potato to every 7lb of bread; rate of extraction 78%
- Butter cost 2s 6d per lb, a cauliflower cost 1s, a tin of peaches 4s 6d, and milk cost 9d per quart
- **November:** potato subsidy
- Lord Mayor of London's banquet took place at time of great hardship
- **December:** over 1,000 people in margarine queue in London
- **Christmas:** seen as the worst experienced so far during war conditions; meat particularly short
- Coal came under government control; queues for coal and food common
- Government appeals for people to adopt voluntary rationing
- The *Eat-Less-Meat Book* (Mrs C.S. Peel) was published, Savings and Savoury Dishes was reissued
- Throwing rice at weddings forbidden, as was using laundry starch; cake shops could sell only 2oz of cake or bread for afternoon tea
- Local Food Controllers were appointed, butchers were ordered to display price lists, bakers were forbidden to bake anything but government bread
- Muffin men disappeared from streets
- Civilians forbidden to give bread to any animals
- Russian wheat no longer imported (Bolshevik Revolution) substitutes, e.g. Sypgar and Consyp, appear in shops
- Annual jam making stopped after 3 sugar ships were sunk

1918

- **1 January:** sugar rationing begins (8oz per head per week), girls aged eighteen and under were paid £1 per week to work in ration-card department

- **28 January:** workers in Manchester demonstrate in favour of compulsory rationing
- **February:** veal no longer for sale
- **11 February:** 'Conscience Week' – amnesty on hoarded food if surrendered by 25 February (fine up to £400)
- **25 February:** government introduces rationing and coupon system used with ration cards, initially in use for margarine and butter
- **March-April:** war bread extraction rate 92% (period of greatest scarcity)
- **7 April:** meat rationing extends to whole country, including the Royal family; by the end of April people had to register to buy bacon
- **Early summer:** fat American bacon appears in shops
- **14 July:** official rationing begins
- **End of July:** German blockade ends
- **September:** cod cost 1s 10d per lb, marmalade 1s per lb, and flour 2½d per lb
- **November:** submarine warfare ends
- **11 November:** Armistice signed
- Publication of the *Victory Cookery Book*

six
Penny Capitalism

During the inter-war period, and more particularly during the Depression years of the 1930s, housewives were encouraged to turn to home-based moneymaking schemes or to attempt to make their hobbies into paying concerns. Working at home was seen as an unobtrusive way to add to the family's income in an era when it would have been a matter of considerable shame for a woman to go out to work because a man was unable to support his family financially. Many jobs were closed to married women at this time, and in *Women in the 1920s*, author Pamela Horn highlights the frustration and boredom felt by those women, formerly in well-paid and skilled jobs, who had been forced to resign on marriage and subsequently resented their 'just a housewife' lives.

The range of money-making schemes detailed in the literature of the period is too wide to cover here in any detail. Some of the ideas included:

- Rearing ferrets, rabbits, ducks, bantams, bees, parrots, lovebirds, canaries, dormice, pheasants, squirrels, silkworms and turkeys. An American magazine carried an eye-catching small ad offering 'Big husky chicks' for sale, but in the UK they would probably have been advertised simply as baby chicks[91]
- Growing cut flowers, herbs, mushrooms, salad crops, vegetables and fruit. One writer felt that money could be made from selling fruit pulp but this idea did not seem to catch on[92]
- Running agencies (insurance, mail order and typing)
- Providing services (hairdressing, doll hospitals, house decoration, handyman/handywoman, gardening, demonstrating goods and appliances in shops, running tea shops and cafés, mending bachelors' socks, and carpentry)
- 'intellectual' (journalism, lecturing, writing, music and painting)

A huge variety of craft ideas was available in the inter-war period. They included popular handicrafts, thrift crafts and the more traditional everyday crafts at which women were assumed to excel. Among the many handicrafts popular during the 1920s and 1930s were:

- Raffia work
- Basketry
- Barbola (modelling with a paste-like substance that could be painted once dry and stuck to small mirrors etc.)
- Bamboo work (kites, fishing rods etc.)
- Chip carving (tools cost between 6d and 1s in the 1930s)
- Doll and teddy bear making and dressing
- Fretwork
- Lace making
- Luffa work (carving loofahs into shapes)
- Marbling
- Naml work (enamel paint brushed onto the raised designs on brass blanks, then varnished – scarf pins and brooches were the items most usually made)
- Needle pictures (using fine wool to outline-stitch features such as trees)
- Novelties: small items for bazaars and sales of work – papier mâché and passe-partout (a style of frame for small pictures)
- Poker work
- Sealing-wax work (sticks of sealing wax were melted using a spirit lamp, shaped into leaves, petals, etc., and stuck to boxes, buttons, picture frames, etc., or attached to vellum or parchment)
- Smocking
- Ribbon work (popular for wedding outfits and favours, including handkerchief sachets, flowers, wedding dresses, etc., and also in the home for underclothes, shoe bags, work bags and curtains were often threaded or decorated with satin ribbon)
- China painting
- Tarso (cutting designs into wood to have the appearance of inlay; also known as intarsia)

The area covered by thrift handicrafts was concerned mostly with finding decorative or functional uses for bits and pieces that probably seemed too good to throw away. It was not an area that promised great financial rewards, but nevertheless hobby guides of the 1930s often included lists of ideas that may well have sparked off inspiration for money making in related areas. They included:

- Bead making (paper beads made by cutting, rolling and sticking thin strips of paper from magazines; cork beads made by cutting corks into thin disks; nut beads made from hazel nuts polished, bored and threaded)

- Book rests made from date boxes
- Cellophane from cigarette packets folded into one inch strips and interlocked to make decorative items such as belts.
- Cigar band craft (sticking cigar bands to plates, vases or ash trays to resemble multicoloured china – this craft depended on large amounts of cigar bands as many were needed to build up the design, but as cigar smoking was not fashionable in the 1930s it was in somewhat of a decline)
- Fishbone ornaments (cod head bones cleaned, dried and carved into shapes – butterflies were said to be popular)
- Flowers (ovals cut from old summer dresses, backed with canvas, attached to pipe cleaners and put in a vase in the sitting room)
- Meat bone ornaments (to hold spills or tapers); knuckle of mutton bones minus meat (cooked and used in recipes) and marrow (used for marrow toast or for baking) are hollow and could be painted jade and silver, blue or crimson, secured on a sealing wax base and set on the mantelpiece; they could also be used as paperweights or toys
- Postage stamp craft (using huge numbers of stamps to decorate boxes, vases etc.)
- Shell flowers
- Twig craft (twigs painted with Chinese lacquer to match a colour scheme. Small bells, shells or balls made from crumpled silver paper and stuck to the twigs were said to be attractive, and they could be sold to shops as ideal additions to window displays)

The more traditional crafts such as metalwork and enamelling, book binding and leather work were perennially popular and frequently appeared in the literature of the period as reliable ways of making money. Although each craft required specific equipment and appropriate training, the 1930s was a decade of do-it-yourself, and basic instruction was given in several household encyclopaedias and hobby guides. Metalwork and enamelling, in particular, remained popular for several decades and featured as a financially viable craft in a range of publications between 1911 and the 1930s. To give one example of set-up costs in 1911, basic equipment comprised:

- an enamelling stove (£5)
- chasing tools
- brush
- pestle and mortar
- enamels (4d per oz)
- gold and silver as needed

In 1911, £5 would buy a good 'costume' or equip (with some money to spare) a small house with china and glass, including kitchen jugs, plates and dishes, plus one dinner service, one breakfast service and a full service of glassware.[93] It was therefore clearly not a craft for anyone on a low income (although Kathleen Dayus records in her autobiography that she trained as a jewellery enameller in Birmingham's Jewellery Quarter during the First World War). Training in metalwork and enamelling could be taken at provincial art colleges such as the Birmingham School of Art or, in London, at Alexander Fisher's studios at 17 Warwick Gardens, Kensington (Alexander Fisher was an influential Arts & Crafts silversmith). After this, the aspiring craftswoman might exhibit her work in London by applying to what must surely be one of the longest titles ever written on an envelope:

The British and Industrial League and United Gentlewomen's
Handicraft and Home Industries Exhibition
42 Vardens Road
London
SW1

Prospects were not wonderful: a designer might, according to *The Woman's Book* (1911) make between £75 and £80 a year.[94] However, metalwork and enamelling remained a popular craft right into the 1930s, perhaps because it was a compact activity requiring little in the way of space and equipment.

Finally, the basic everyday crafts such as knitting, crochet, embroidery, dressmaking and millinery were included in many books, but as women were assumed to be competent knitters it was perhaps inevitable that the market was overcrowded and demand was small. In addition, many women owned knitting machines, and magazines offered prizes for the best 'woollies' and ran adverts describing how women could make large amounts of money supplying knitwear to the knitting machine companies. Small, simple garments for babies and young children could be made fairly quickly while higher prices could be demanded for more complex designs. Kathleen Dayus's autobiography referred to a woman who made a small business out of unravelling old knitted garments and making gloves and scarves to sell. The knitter would need to corner the market by producing either something very special or very intricate. Regional specialities such as Shetland shawls, once popular for babies, were still prized in the 1930s but were beginning to be seen as old-fashioned by a younger generation of mothers who favoured machine-made items such as the pram rugs made by Otterburn. Machine-made pram rugs were much easier to wash and took far less trouble to 'do up' than hand-knitted shawls, which had to be stretched out on the floor to dry overnight with all points and lace edges carefully pinned out.

Crochet was also very popular, with thread manufacturers running competitions and various third-party organisations offering to sell completed work. Most women could crochet and there were many patterns for both thread (lace for doyleys and tablecloths) and wool (pram covers and jumpers). However, crochet uses up wool far more quickly than knitting does so from a thrift point of view it may well have been kept for 'best' or special projects such as christening shawls.

Kits and patterns were available for those who preferred (and could afford) to buy them. During the 1920s and 1030s they included rug making (Readicut), cane work (Dryad), sewing and embroidery (Coats, Singer), and knitting (Best Way, Weldon's). Many homes had sewing machines, and knitting machines generally came with directions and patterns for simple items. Patterns were also available in magazines and through the commercial patterns sold in handicraft shops. Patterns such as these had the advantage of illustrations: instructions in home sewing books were sometimes difficult to follow because of the poor quality (or total lack) of illustrations.

Magazines such as *Good Needlework* and *Knitting Magazine*, *Woman's Weekly*, and *Woman & Home* included regular features on knitting, embroidery and dressmaking, with transfers for copying patterns, photos and drawings to illustrate techniques, and hints on colour schemes and materials. Another way to pick up a new craft was by attending a course, although this was not a route open to all women. However, organisations such as the Women's Institute offered courses in basket making, and crafts such as upholstering were available at various polytechnics and technical schools around the country.

Many women took up dressmaking, providing an essential service at a time when women did not usually buy clothes readymade. Trimmings such as feathers, lace and ribbons could be added with varying degrees of taste and style by a 'little dressmaker' who might also do alterations or repairs, take up hems or make the odd summer frock. Women who had 'clever fingers' and could trim or remodel hats were in demand, and many little shops (some sited in back parlours of houses and villas) survived on the trade of millinery and clothes alteration.

Another home-based utility craft was quilting. Women in South Wales and the North of England had a long-standing tradition of making and selling wholecloth and 'strippy' quilts, and in the 1920s and 1930s many of these communities had a tradition of 'quilt clubs'. Members paid a small sum into a kitty over a period of several weeks to cover materials and labour, and then drew lots to see who would receive the completed quilt. Then they would draw lots for the next one, and so on. Quilt making is quite obtrusive, compared to other needlework crafts, as a quilting frame needs a great deal of space, but it was a very popular means of making some money at a time when many men were unemployed or on short time. For more information, see Dorothy Osler, *Traditional British Quilts* (Batsford, 1987).

Many households in mill areas made rugs from oddments from the factories, known as 'fents'. Rugs could be made on looms, but many were made by 'prodding' small pieces or pushing strips into sacking to form patterns or pictures, or by knotting small lengths of wool onto canvas with a special tool known as a latch hook. Firms such as Readicut supplied kits, wool and patterns for rug craft and many households had a fireside rug made this way. Materials were easy to find, as sacking was easily available, and worn-out clothes were habitually saved for patching or making rugs. The completed rug would migrate around the house, starting as a 'best' in front of the sitting room fire and eventually ending up in the dog's basket, by which time another rug had embarked on an identical trip around the house – nothing was wasted that could be used somewhere.

Food and Domestic-Based Schemes

Inevitably, many of the money-making schemes aimed at housewives involved food, cooking or housework. Most of these activities needed space, equipment and some financial outlay, so they were more likely to be popular with women living in the type of house that had storage space to spare as well as money for the ingredients and the various pieces of equipment to make sweets or bake cakes. Sweet making in particular required a solid business brain, an artistic eye, neat fingers and useful social connections, as well as training in the various areas such as sugar boiling. Courses in 1911 cost about 10s 6d per lesson (the same price as a good wire mattress or a set of fire-irons) so access was probably limited to the middle classes or those cooks sent by their mistresses to learn a new skill.[95] Start-up costs included around £10 for packaging, moulds and small implements such as a sugar thermometer (approximately 4s 6d), a marble slab, some strong saucepans, a wire fork and ring, greaseproof paper and small boxes. This outlay was a heavy one for anyone but the well-heeled: a small house could be kitted out with sixty-nine articles of kitchenware for just over £6 in 1911. Refined elegant packaging was essential, the example to follow in 1911 being Fullers, who packed their sweets in white paper and white boxes wrapped with tasteful coloured ribbon. Prospects were said to be very good, especially if the sweet-maker had an extensive list of friends and connections willing to buy her wares on a regular basis. Sweet-makers were encouraged to start in a modest way with basic recipes such as brandy cherries coated with fondant, before launching into jellies and caramels and the more ambitious recipes.

The housewife wishing to make the occasional batch of sweets for the children or visitors could follow recipes in cookery books, combining a treat with thrifty use of leftovers such as crystallised orange rinds. This recipe made use of orange peel by cutting it into thin strips, dipping it in sugar syrup and rolling it in caster sugar.[96] A variety of sweets could be made 'uncooked', meaning a small saving in fuel, but these were not suitable for selling because of their short shelf life. However, the resourceful housewife could probably get around this by selling them at bazaars and sales of work which were hugely popular in the 1930s, or by using them as experimental recipes to serve to the family. Uncooked fondant (far easier to make than the cooked sort) made lemon, orange and ginger creams, and marzipan could be made into potato, strawberry and pear shapes.

A 1930s recipe for meat extract jujubes succeeded in combining cooking, nutrition, thrift and the ability to miss a day's meals with no ill effect: the jujubes comprised meat extract and lemon jelly, salt and pepper, and was cut into small cubes. A handful of these plus a handful of an alternative variety made with port wine, plus a couple of apples, were recommended as an easy portable meal for a day out. The idea for this portable food may have come via a product marketed by Nelson's as 'Hipi' Lozenges and advertised in the 1903 edition of *Home Comforts* (few people seemed to bother about stealing other people's ideas, a fact borne out by the plethora of hints and tips copied from one book and used in another). Hipi Lozenges were said to be ideal for travellers, invalids and cyclists alike, especially handy because they did not contain salt and would therefore not make the consumer thirsty.[97]

Another occupation said to be ideal for housewives was baking and selling cakes. The growth and proliferation of teashops, cafés and roadhouses in the 1930s was linked in part with the increased number of private cars on the roads and the new-found interest in hiking and rambling. Hungry travellers (if they had not armed themselves with handfuls of jujubes) always needed food. The woman who could spot a gap in the market, show a selection of her wares to demonstrate her skills, organise prompt and efficient delivery (one book refers to a delivery method involving a boy with a box tricycle), keep to a reliable schedule and have a good back-up system in case of emergencies or disasters, would very likely have got herself firmly into a niche market.[98] Packaged bakery products were available but homemade was always popular – the majority of cookery books contained cake recipes and many middle-class teatimes and 'At Homes' invariably featured cake in one form or another.

Prior market research was essential: seaside towns with plenty of holidaymakers in the summer season, market towns with busy teashops and villages with a few passing ramblers all had their different requirements. Dainty cakes and pastries went down better with lady shoppers than with farmers, and hunks of fruit cake were more sustaining than tiny fairy cakes. Premises had to be big enough to cope with plenty of storage and cooling space, preferably a good-sized oven (1930s ovens look very small compared to modern ones), and enough space for a variety of attractive packaging. A reliable oven was essential, and the Vulcan Stove Co. offered a gas oven with a glass door, ideal for baking (opening an oven door to check on progress frequently spelled disaster for the contents).

A course in business practice was recommended (this would have eliminated women without spare money) plus a thorough knowledge of the ins and outs of baking: failures could be expensive, although most could be absorbed by the family dog or any nearby children. The Good Housekeeping Institute ran courses in many branches of cookery, with Florence Jack, one of the early editors of the *Good Housekeeping* magazine, writing articles and cookery books under the Good Housekeeping name. The Women's

Institute organised competitions and encouraged members to adopt a professional attitude in their work: this in turn raised standards and ensured the continuing success of the WI (see Penny Kitchen, *For Home and Country*, Leopard Books, 1996).

As women were expected to be able to cook (and public opinion also assumed that they enjoyed doing it), occupations such as catering were seen as ideal money spinners. Acting as something between a servant, a waitress and a housekeeper, the caterer would draw up dinner party menus and provide lists of supplies (but not do the shopping herself), and then do the cooking and dishing up (but not the sink work, clearing up or washing up). 5s per engagement was seen as a reasonable sum to charge in the early 1930s and a successful woman could advertise her services in newspapers and make herself available for birthdays, wedding receptions and similar celebrations. This type of arrangement was probably ideal for households without servants and with busy social lives, or those where a lot of entertaining went on, and ideal also for women with a wide circle of friends but neither the time nor inclination to do her own cooking.

Finally, if the housewife found herself in a situation that necessitated complete overhaul of her life, she could emigrate to the Colonies. Clearly this was not an opportunity available to everyone, but in 1911 emigration to Canada or South Africa was seen as an ideal next step for the woman keen to use her domestic skills in new and (hopefully) exciting circumstances. Childless widows with no ties or, after the First World War, the women who never married and were known as 'surplus women', as well as those with a simple sense of adventure, were said to be ideal candidates for emigration. Skills in housewifery, agriculture and horticulture could be learnt at Swanley Horticultural College, Stoke Prior Colonial Training College or Arlesley Training College. A twelve-month course at Arlesley cost £80 with courses in driving, carpentry and bee-keeping as well as the more everyday domestic subjects. As a small flat could be furnished for 90 guineas in 1911 this was a serious amount of money, but female emigrants could expect to earn far more than those who stayed at home.[99]

By the 1930s training in domestic activities was still being pushed at young women. Housekeeping – as anyone who does it knows – is endless, thankless and boring, but at the same time there is a certain pleasure to be got from a clean, comfortable, well-kept home. Of course, someone has to do the work to keep it that way. Housekeeping on a shoestring, shopping carefully and cooking economically is much easier these days but conversely we seem to take far less pride in domestic skills such as cooking and cleaning. Few people would wish to return to the days when women had to divide up their housekeeping money by allocating pennies to meat, fruit and vegetables, or spend hours scrubbing floors and hauling heavy washing around, but skills once lost are often skills that disappear for good, and thrift is a skill learned more by experience than example.

Conclusion

Housekeepers have always had to 'cut their coats according to the cloth' and those on small or fixed budgets have struggled with rising prices and the need to provide nutritious meals for their families through wars, shortages and food scares. This book is a very small window into the past, revealing some of the thrift ideas offered to housewives over a thirty-year period of social and economic upheaval, but also highlighting the difficulties they faced in the most rudimentary areas of domestic life such as feeding and clothing their families on insufficient money.

Anyone who reads old cookery books begins to explore the background of the times, whether the mock food of the war years, the sheep's head and ox tongue dishes of the 1930s or the elaborate dishes 'done up' to disguise their humble origins. They may also begin to ponder the fact that housewives had a huge legacy of frugality and economy at their fingertips that has almost completely disappeared. Modern life is less sympathetic to brushing up breadcrumbs or saving fish trimmings and the other thrift strategies that were practiced by necessity in former times, and it is debatable whether anyone would want to extend the life of a bath sponge by six years or find uses for tagless boot laces. Modern shopping methods relying on supermarkets have removed the need to keep 'emergency' store cupboards and to buy coffee in tiny amounts, but conversely they have made us a nation of passive shoppers, happy to buy what is offered and less and less able to live on our culinary wits. Housewives are rarely seen as heroes, but surely anyone who performs miracles with food and cooking year in year out, keeps a clean, organised and happy home and raises her family to the best of her ability on minimal amounts of money is a hero indeed.

Glossary

Alum	mineral salt with astringent and drying properties, used in dyeing, tanning and reproofing of garments
Bath brick	brick made form mix of sand and clay, used for scouring
Boracic acid/ boric acid	mineral used as antiseptic, preservative and in industry
Burgundy pitch	obtained from the Norway spruce
Coal briquettes	coal dust mixed with clay and moulded into small balls, sold under brand name Ovoid in the early twentieth century
Ox gall	purified ox bile; used as a laxative and antiseptic in the early twentieth century
Pipeclay	white clay used by the military for whitening leather
Plumbago	alternative name for graphite; used as a lubricant
Pumice stone	solidified lava; used as an abrasive cleaning material
Puttees	long narrow bands of woollen or other material worn by soldiers; wrapped around the legs in spiral fashion, they were said to offer protection, reduce the likelihood of varicose veins and be warmer than leggings
Red lead	used in plumbing and as a paint primer and pigment; now known to be toxic
Sal ammoniac	aluminium chloride; used as a vapour inhalant (more commonly known as smelling salts) and to make the electrolyte in batteries in the 1930s
Spirits of turpentine	volatile oil of turpentine
Spirits of wine	ordinary alcohol
Sugar of lead	lead acetate
Sulphurous acid	used as an antiseptic, deodorant and disinfectant in the 1930s
Vermilion	red pigment derived from cinnabar
Water-glass	solution of silicate of soda and water, boiled and then cooled; used to preserve eggs bought when they were cheap against the winter when

they were not always available in the shops – the
eggs were dipped and then dried, the water-
glass forming a film on the shells. The eggs could
either be kept in the water-glass or stored on
shelves or special racks

White lead   much used in paint in the 1930s; now known to
be toxic

Notes

1.Humble, *Culinary Pleasures*, p. 34

2.Orwell, *The Road to Wigan Pier*, p. 86

3.Crawford, *People's Food*, p. 112

4.'Report of the Committee appointed to Enquire into and report upon (i) the actual increase since June, 1914, in the Cost of Living to the working classes', p. 18

5.Crawford, p. 129

6.Cole & Cole, *The Condition of Britain*, p. 61

7.Minter, *Book of the Home*, Vol. 1, Table A, p. 115

8.Barker, *Christ in the Valley of Unemployment*, p. 32

9.Craig, *Economical Cookery*, p. 11

10.Greenwood, *How the Other Man Lives*, p. 129

11.Minter, Vol. 1, Table B, 116

12.Wilson, *Co-operative Managers' Text Book*, p. 135

13.*Birmingham Daily Post*, December 13, 1894

14.*Book of Hints & Wrinkles*, p. 184

15.Ibid., 124-125

16.Ibid., p. 185

17.Cole & Cole, p. 127

18.Jack, *Cookery for Every Household*, p. 24

19.Williams, *Best Butter in the World*, p. 35

20.*Housewife's Book*, p. 14

21.*Enquire Within*, p. 326

22.Ibid., pp. 325-326

23.Wilson, chapter XXV

24.*Concise Household Encyclopaedia*, Vol. 1, p. 479

25.*Home Cookery & Comforts*, November 1913 issue, pp. 319-320

26.Garth & Wrench, *Home Management*, pp. 484-488

27.Waller, *Emelie Waller's Cookery & Kitchen Book for Slender Purses*, p. 7

28.Craig, *Economical Cookery*, pp. 11-14

29.Garth & Wrench, *Home Management*, p. 485

30.*Complete Illustrated Household Encyclopaedia*, p. 531

31.Burnett, *Plenty & Want*, p. 213

32.*Concise Household Encyclopaedia*, Vol. 2, 1297

33.*Housewife's Book*, p. 15

34.Struan, *Popular Home Cookery*, p. 51

35.Stote, *Bride's Book*, 137

36.Ibid., ill 161

37.*Home Cookery & Comforts*, November 1913 issue, p. 336

38.Ibid., p. 351, 333

39.*You & I Cookery Book*, p. 18, 31, 15

40.*Tried Favourites*, p. 17, 62, 129, 138

41.*Best Way*, book 1, p. 35, 55, 58

42.Waller, *Emelie Waller's Cookery & Kitchen Book for Slender Purses*, p. 82

43.Francillon & G.T.C.D.S, *Good Cookery*, p. 19

44.White, *Good Things in England*, p. 106, 210, 298

45.Craig, *Economical Cookery*, p. 135, 11, 36

46.*Economical Cookery*, chapter XV

47.*You & I Cookery Book*, p. 39, 8, 12; *Tried Favourites*, p. 7; *Best Way*, book 4, p. 65

48.Hartley, *Food in England*, p. 90

49.*Best Way*, book 1, pp. 61-63

50.*Best Way*, book 4, 60; You & I Cookery Book, p. 8, 39, 40, 54, 57, 59, 149,

51.Hooper, *Nelson's Home Comforts*, p. 52, 72

52.*Tried Favourites*, pp. 213-216

53.Ibid., pp. 221-223

54.*Home Cookery & Comforts*, November 1913 issue, p. 343

55.Ibid., pp. 343-344

56.*Tried Favourites*, p. 278

57.Ibid., p. 233

58.Humphry, *Book of the Home*, Vol. 3, p. 80

59.Wise, *Round-the-Clock Cookery Book 1935*, pp. 124-129

60.*Bestway Cookery Gift Book* No. 5, p. 127

61.*Home Cookery & Comforts*, November 1913 issue, p. 325

62.*Best Way*, Book 4, p. 37

63.Craig, *Economical Cookery*, p. 201

64.Marshall, p. 70

65.*Best Way*, Vol. 4, p. 20

66.Humphry, p. 125

67.Beddoe, *Discovering Women's History*, illustration 10; Jack, *Cookery for Every Household*, p. 626

68.*Tried Favourites*, p. 276

69.*Home Words*, p. 112

70.Ryan & Ryan, *Dinners for Beginners*, p. 67

71.Peel, *Learning to Cook*, p. 177

72.Ibid., p. 182

73.*Home Cookery & Comforts*, November 1913 issue, p. 325

74.Marshall, *Newnes Everything Within*, p. 216

75.Humphry, p. 123

76.*Enquire Within*, p. 100

77.*You & I Cookery Book*, p. 97

78.Greenwood, p. 123

79.*National Food Economy League Handbook for Housewives*, p. 3

80.Sharp, *Temperance Pioneer 1907*, p. 201

81.Report of the Committee, p. 7

82.Pankhurst, *The Home Front*, p. 337

83.*National Food Economy League Handbook for Housewives*, 40+, back cover

84.Peel & Kriens, *Victory Cook Book*, p. 236

85.Peel, *How We Lived Then*, Appendix XI

86.*National Food Economy League Handbook for Housewives*, p. 9

87.*Savings & Savoury Dishes*, p. 39

88.Peel & Kriens, p. 227-228

89.Peel, p. 212

90.Ibid. p. 208

91.*Needlecraft*, March 1931 issue, p. 30

92.Byron, *May Byron's Jam Book*, p. 3

93.Jack & Strauss, *Woman's Book*, p. 37

94.Jack & Strauss, p. 689

95.Ibid., p. 671

96.*Bestway Cookery Gift Book*, Book 6, p. 153

97.Hooper, *Nelson's Home Comforts*, p. 8

98.Marshall, p. 580

99.Jack & Strauss, p. 661

Bibliography

Barker, R.J., *Christ in the Valley of Unemployment* (Hodder & Stoughton: London, 1936)

Beddoe, Deirdre, *Discovering Women's History* (Pandora: London, 1983)

Beeton, Isabella, *Mrs Beeton's Cookery Book* (Ward Lock: London, 1913)

Best Way number 1 (Amalgamated Press: London, no date)

Best Way number 4 (Amalgamated Press: London, no date)

Bestway Cookery Gift Book, 5th Book (Bestway: London, no date)

Bestway Cookery Gift Book, 6th Book (Bestway: London, no date)

Book of Hints and Wrinkles (Odhams: London, no date)

Breck, Mrs Alan, *The Mrs Alan Breck Recipe Book* (Cooper & Co: Glasgow, 1921)

Burnett, John, *Plenty and Want* (Routledge: London, 1985)

Byron, May, *May Byron's Jam Book* (Hodder & Stoughton, London, no date)

Cairns, Julia, *Re-Dress your Rooms* (Singer Sewing Machine Co: London, 1938)

Cole, G.D.H. and Cole, M.I., *The Condition of Britain* (Left Book Club: London, 1937)

Concise Household Encyclopedia , Vols 1-2, (Amalgamated Press, London, no date)

Cooking by Gas (B.C.G.A.: London, no date)

Cottington-Taylor, D.D (foreword), *Vulcan Cook Book* (Vulcan Stove Co: London, 1936)

Craig, Elizabeth, *Economical Cookery* (Collins: London, 1934)

Crawford, William, *The People's Food* (Heinemann: London, 1937)

Dayus, Kathleen, *Where There's Life* (Virago: London, 1985)

Economical Cookery and Menus for Every Day in the Year (foreword D.D. Cottington-Taylor) (*Daily Express*: London, no date)

Enquire Within, 106th edn (Madgwick & Houlston: London, 1910)

Fairclough, M.A., *Ideal Cookery Book* (Blackfriars: London, no date)

Fairclough, M.A., *Lloyd's Practical Household Management* (*Lloyd's Weekly News*: London, 1913)

Four Hundred Prize Recipes for Practical Cookery (*Daily Telegraph*: London, no date)

Francillon, W.G.R. and G.T.C.D.S., *Good Cookery* (J.M. Dent: London, 1946)

Garth, Molly and Wrench, Mrs Stanley, *Home Management* (*Daily Express*: London, 1934)

Graham, Eleanor, *The Children who Lived in a Barn* (Puffin / Penguin: London, 1938)

Greenwood, Walter, *How the Other Man Lives* (Labour Book Service: London, no date)

Hartley, Dorothy, *Food in England* (Macdonald & Jane's: London, 1954)

Heaton, Nell, *Complete Cook* (Marrray's Sales and Service / Cresta: London, no date)

Home Cookery & Comforts November 1913 (C. Arthur Pearson: London, 1913)

Home Cookery & Comforts July 1914 (C. Arthur Pearson: London, 1914)

Home Words (Home Words: London, no date)

Hooper, Mary, *Nelson's Home Comforts, 22nd revised enlarged edn* (C. Nelson Dale & Co: London, 1903)

Horn, Pamela, *Women in the 1920s* (Alan Sutton: Stroud, 1995)

Housewife's Book (*Daily Express*: London, no date)

Humble, Nicola, *Culinary Pleasures* (Faber: London, 2005)

Humphry, Mrs C.E. ('Madge' of 'Truth'), *Book of the Home*, Vol. 3 (Gresham: London, 1909)

Jack, Florence B., *Cookery for Every Household* (T.C. & E.C. Jack: London, 1914)

Jack, Florence B., *Herbert's Book of Casserole Cookery* (Newnes: London, no date)

Jack, Florence B. and Strauss, Rita (eds), *The Woman's Book* (T.C. & E.C. Jack: London, 1911)

Kirk, Mrs E.W., *Tried Favourites* (Fairgrieve: Edinburgh, no date)

Kitchen, Penny, *For Home and Country: the W.I. Magazine 1919-1959* (Leopard: London, 1996)

Lees-Dods, Matilda, *The Ideal Home: How to Find It, How to Furnish It, How to Keep It* (Waverley Book Co: London, no date)

M'Gonigle, G.C.M. and Kirby, J., *Poverty and Public Health* (Left Book Club: London, 1936)

Marshall, A.C., (ed.), *Newnes Everything Within* (Newnes: London, no date)

Minter, Davide C. (ed), *Book of the Home*, 4 Vols. (Gresham: London, 1927)

National Food Economy League Handbook for Housewives, 10th edn (NFEL: London, no date)

Needlecraft: the Magazine of Home Arts Augusta, Maine, USA, issue March 1931

Neil, Marion Harris, *Thrift Cook Book* (David McKay: Philadelphia, 1919)

Orr, John Boyd, *Food, health and Income, 2nd edn* (Macmillan: London, 1937)

Orr, John Boyd, *National Food Supply and its Influence on Public Health* (text of lecture given to the Chadwick Institute: London, 1934)

Orwell, George, *The Road to Wigan Pier* (Penguin: London, 1987. First published 1937)

Osler, Dorothy, *Traditional British Quilts* (Batsford: London, 1987)

Pankhurst, E. Sylvia, *The Home Front* (Cresset Library: London, 1987. First published 1932)

Peel, Mrs C.S., *Daily Mail Cookery Book, 4th edn* (*Daily Mail*: London, 1920)

Peel, Mrs C.S., *Eat-Less-Meat Book: War Ration Housekeeping* (John Lane: London, 1917)

Peel, Mrs C.S., *How we Lived Then,* (John Lane: London, 1929)

Peel, Mrs C.S., *Learning to Cook* (Constable: London, 1915)

Peel, Mrs C.S. and Kriens, Iwan, *Victory Cookery Book* (John Lane: London, 1918)

Reeves, Maud Pember, *Round About a Pound a Week* (Virago: London, 1979. First published 1913)

Rice, Margery Spring, *Working-Class Wives* (Virago: London, 1981. First published 1939)

Rohde, Eleanour Sinclair, *Haybox Cookery* (George Routledge: London, 1939)

Ryan, Rachel and Margaret, *Dinners for Beginners* (Hamish Hamilton: London, 1934)

Sam Smith, Grocer Extraordinary (Kellogg Company of Great Britain: London, no date)

Savings and Savoury Dishes (A & C Black: London, 1917)

Sharp, Revd J. Alfred (ed), *Temperance Pioneer*, Vol. 1, 1907 (Robert Culley: London, 1907)

Silburn, Judith Ann, *Readers Library Cookery Book* (Readers Library Publishing Co.: London, no date)

Silvester, Elizabeth, *Silvester's Sensible Cookery* (Herbert Jenkins: London, no date)

Simmonds, W.H., *The Practical Grocer*, Vol. 1 (Gresham: London, 1904)

Stote, Dorothy, *Bride's Book* (Bride's Book Co: London, no date)

Struan, Margaret, *Popular Home Cookery.* (Pitman, 1935)

Waller, Emelie, *Emelie Waller's Cookery and Kitchen Book for Slender Purses* (Faber: London, 1935)

White, Florence, *Good Things in England* (Futura: London, 1974. First published 1932)

Wilkinson, Mrs, *Mrs Wilkinson's Cookery Book* (Simpkin, Marshall, Hamilton, Kent & Co: London, no date)

Williams, Bridget, *The Best Butter in the World* (Ebury Press: London, 1994)

Wilson, R.J. (ed), *Co-operative Managers' Text Book* (Co-operative Union: Manchester, 1915)

Wise, Mrs: *'Round-the-Clock' Cookery Book 1935* (Amalgamated Press: London, 1935)

Working Classes Cost of Living Committee, 1918, 'Report of the Committee Appointed to Enquire into and Report upon(i) the Actual Increase in the Cost of Living to the Working Classes and (ii) any Counterbalancing Factors (apart from increases of wages) which may have Arisen under War Conditions' (H.M.S.O.: London, 1918)

You & I Cookery Book (Birling Publishing Co: Birling, Kent, no date)

Index

Other titles published by The History Press

The Workhouse Cookbook

PETER HIGGINBOTHAM

This evocative book explores every aspect of life – and diet – in the workhouse. With more than 100 photographs, recipes, plans and dietary tables, it is a shocking, surprising and utterly unique guide to one of the most notorious establishments of the past. *The Workhouse Cookbook* will delight cooks, epicureans and lovers of history everywhere.

978 0 7524 4730 8

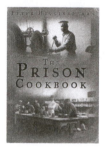

The Prison Cookbook

PETER HIGGINBOTHAM

This richly illustrated book examines the history of prison catering from the Middle Ages to the present day. With sections on prison life, punishments, the food on board transportation vessels, and the work of reformers such as John Howard and Elizabeth Fry, this evocative and unique book shows the reader exactly what 'doing porridge' entailed.

978 0 7524 5423 8

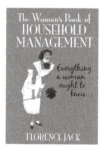

The Woman's Book of Household Management

FLORENCE JACK

In the distant past, when a Lady had servants, she relied on *The Woman's Book,* a weighty tome full of useful information and tips on how to run her household. With everything from the price of setting up and furnishing a new home to how to clean, remove stains, and generally run a house in the Edwardian period.

978 0 7524 4210 5

Spuds, Spam and Eating for Victory

KATHERINE KNIGHT

The rationing of food, clothing and other substances played a big part in making sure that everyone had a fair share of whatever was available during the Second World War. In this fascinating book, Katherine Knight looks at how experiences of rationing varied between rich and poor, town and country, and how ingenuous cooks often made a meal from poor ingredients.

978 0 7524 4188 7

Visit our website and discover thousands of other History Press books.

www.thehistorypress.co.uk

Lightning Source UK Ltd.
Milton Keynes UK
UKOW07f0219141114

241576UK00001B/9/P